Economics of Feeding the Hungry

As productivity expands to cater for ̦ ̦ulation increase and shifting diets, many individuals remain hungry, whilst others suffer obesity, and significant amounts of food are wasted. Yet, this triple dilemma oversimplifies the underlying complexity of the global food system. This book explores this complexity from an economics perspective, looking at the processes involved and the institutional structures that direct and constrain their interaction.

After discussing alternative approaches to measuring hunger and food insecurity, this volume considers the four dimensions of food security: availability, affordability, utilisation and stability. In summarising the main debates, issues and policy interventions, Russell discusses the problems of ensuring sufficient food in the face of ever-slowing growth in productivity and constraints on land and water. The problems of food affordability, the need for safety nets and the need for poverty alleviation measures that reach excluded and disadvantaged groups are also discussed. This is alongside an exploration of issues related to food utilisation and the problems of hidden hunger, obesity, food waste and the interventions needed to relieve these problems.

This volume is of great interest to those who study rural development, ecological economics and development economics, as well as policy makers who seek a better understanding of underlying processes, ongoing and emerging issues and potentially relevant interventions.

Noel Russell is a Senior Lecturer of Agricultural and Environmental Economics at the University of Manchester, UK. His research interests are centred on economic analysis of policies for farming, food and rural resources.

Routledge Studies in Ecological Economics

For a full list of titles in this series, please visit www.routledge.com/series/RSEE

Economics of Feeding the Hungry

Sustainable Intensification and Sustainable Food Security

Noel Russell

LONDON AND NEW YORK

First published 2018
by Routledge

2 Park Square, Milton Park, Abingdon, Oxfordshire OX14 4RN
52 Vanderbilt Avenue, New York, NY 10017

Routledge is an imprint of the Taylor & Francis Group, an informa business

First issued in paperback 2019

British Library Cataloguing-in-Publication Data
A catalogue record for this book is available from the British Library

Library of Congress Cataloging-in-Publication Data
A catalog record for this book has been requested

ISBN: 978-0-415-53858-9 (hbk)
ISBN: 978-0-367-34107-7 (pbk)

Typeset in Times New Roman
by Apex CoVantage, LLC

To Margaret, Catherine, Elaine and Patrick, to Aaron, Andrew and Alice, and to all my grandchildren

Contents

Figures

Tables

Acknowledgements

I would like to thank Seamus Grimes, Sanzidur Rahman and Iain Fraser for their helpful comments and suggestions on various drafts of this book. However, I take sole responsibility for the outcome; I alone am responsible for whatever problems or deficiencies remain.

I would also like to convey my thanks and appreciation to my colleagues in the Economics Department and in the School of Social Sciences at the University of Manchester, who allowed me a generous sabbatical leave that greatly facilitated the completion of this book.

Finally, I would like to say a special thanks to Andy Humphries, Emily Kindleysides, Laura Johnson and all the team at Routledge.

Abbreviations

CFS	Committee on World Food Security
CRS	Catholic Relief Services
FAO	Food and Agricultural Organisation of the United Nations
FAOSTAT	Food and Agricultural Organisation of the United Nations Statistics Division
FEWSNET	Famine Early Warning System Network
GHI	Global Hunger Index
GDP	Gross Domestic Product
HLPE	High Level Panel of Experts on Food Security and Nutrition
IFAD	International Fund for Agricultural Development
IFPRI	International Food Policy Research Institute
IPCC	Intergovernmental Panel on Climate Change
MDG	Millennium Development Goals
MEA	Millennium Ecosystem Assessment
OECD	Organisation for Economic Cooperation and Development
PoU	Prevalence of Undernourishment
PPP	Purchasing Power Parity
SDG	Sustainable Development Goals
SUN	Scaling Up Nutrition
TFP	Total Factor Productivity
UN	United Nations
UNICEF	United Nations Children's Fund
USAID	United States Agency for International Development
WCED	World Commission on Environment and Development
WFP	World Food Programme
WFS	World Food Summit
WHO	World Health Organization

1 Introduction

The problems of hunger and malnutrition remain a major concern for many millions of people worldwide. Yet, there has been significant progress in solving these problems as the number of hungry people in the world has declined steadily. Projected to reach an estimated 795 million in 2014–16 (FAO et al., 2015), the number has fallen by around 21 per cent since 1990–92, while the percentage of people who are hungry has fallen from 23 per cent to around 13 per cent in 2014–16.

These numbers are particularly significant since they measure progress in achieving two internationally agreed targets for hunger reduction over the period 1990–92 to 2014–16. At the World Food Summit (WFS) in 1996, 182 countries agreed ". . . to eradicate hunger in all countries, with an immediate view of reducing the number of undernourished people to half their present level no later than 2015"(World Food Summit, 1996). This target envisaged reducing the number of hungry people to around 500 million by 2015, substantially less than the 795 million actually achieved. The second target derives from the Millennium Development Goals (MDG) arising from a pledge by 189 countries in 2000 to provide every individual across the world with basic human rights that include freedom from hunger and deprivation. The first goal, MDG#1, included among its targets that of cutting by half by 2015 the proportion of people suffering from hunger (United Nations, 2014) This target envisaged reducing the prevalence of hunger to just over 11.5 per cent, just below the 12.9 per cent actually achieved.[1]

The fact that both these targets have been missed makes it essential that we re-examine what has happened and seek a new understanding of processes involved and their interactions (Shoaf Kozak et al., 2012). We present this book as one more step in this re-examination where we focus primarily on economic aspects of this problem.

In particular, we consider how we might make more substantive progress in the context of the next set of international goals, the Sustainable Development Goals (SDG), launched in January 2016 (General Assembly on Sustainable Development Goals, 2014). These comprise an integrated set of 17 goals and 169 targets, to be achieved by 2030, that are designed to build on the Millennium Development Goals and seek to complete what they did not achieve (FAO et al., 2015; United Nations Research Institute for Social Development, 2016). The first two SDGs are particularly relevant here. SDG#1 is focused on "ending poverty in all its forms everywhere" and has specific targets to eradicate extreme poverty (living on less than $1.25 per day), and to reduce by half the proportion of men, women and children of all ages living in poverty in all its dimensions by this date. SDG#2 is focused on achieving zero hunger and includes among its targets to ensure access by all people, especially poor people in vulnerable situations, to safe, nutritious and sufficient food all year round, and to end malnutrition in all its forms.

This is in the context of the evident success of attempts to expand productivity of the food production system and its ability to provide sufficient food for our expanding population and shifting diets. At the same time, a significant cohort of individuals are prone to obesity and to the diseases associated with this problem. And there are many examples of where hunger and obesity arise together in the same country and region and even in the same towns and cities. In addition, significant amounts of edible food are wasted by wholesalers, retailers and especially by households. Yet, this triple dilemma of hunger in the face of adequate production, obesity and starvation in the same city and ever-increasing food waste, is an oversimplification of the complex interactions that underpin our food production and consumption activities and the continuing problems with food and nutrition security. Here we explore this complexity from an economics perspective, looking at a number of the principal processes involved and the social and institutional structures that direct and constrain these processes and how they interact. We consider both the significance of problems and issues arising from continuing failure to feed those who are hungry and malnourished, and the effectiveness of proposed interventions, emphasising that the impact of these problems falls mainly on individual people and on the families and households to which they belong.

In pursuing these arguments, we begin by exploring the current state of food security across the world (Chapter 2) as we try to establish the scale of the hunger problem and identify the characteristics of those who are hungry. Here, we discuss the concept and measurement of food security, the ongoing debate around alternative approaches to measurement, and the problems of data availability. For the remaining chapters, we use the four dimensions of food and nutrition security (FAO, 2008) as the basic framework for our discussion.

The food availability dimension addresses the sufficiency of food supply and the capacity of the global food system to deliver increases in productivity to keep pace with increases in global population, changing diets induced by increased prosperity and other factors, and expanding non-food demands arising from biofuel mandates and other changes. We discuss these issues in Chapter 3.

The food affordability (or food entitlements) dimension addresses issues arising for individuals when they are not able to obtain the food they need in the market even when there are adequate amounts of food available. The point being emphasised here is that food security is about being able to consume food, not just that food is available for consumption. This shifts the focus from food production to more general issues related to the livelihoods of consumers, the social dynamics of food distribution, and the behaviour of markets. Chapter 4 explores these issues in more detail.

The food utilisation and nutrition dimension takes the analysis one step further by highlighting the importance of ensuring that the food available in the household is used to best advantage in providing adequate and appropriate nutrition for household members. This brings into focus the education and training of household members and their knowledge of nutrition and hygiene. The facilities available and, the availability of clean water and sanitation infrastructure, are also important. The ability to control the amount of food loss and waste, the problems of hidden hunger and poor nutrition and the income-related transitions to obesity and lifestyle diseases are also considered. In addition, we discuss policy interventions for relieving hidden hunger, alternative approaches for encouraging dietary change, and a range of interventions to reduce food loss and waste across the food value chain. These are the subject of Chapter 5.

The final dimension, focusing on stability, sustainability and resilience of factors underpinning availability, affordability and utilisation, is discussed in Chapter 6. Here we consider food price spikes and interventions to reduce food price volatility. We also investigate the sustainability of food availability and of individual livelihoods, focusing in particular on the role of sustainable intensification. We also investigate recent work on resilience of the food and nutrition system and options to reduce its vulnerability to shocks and stresses.

The final chapter then presents a summary of the main issues discussed and the main findings of this study, and discusses the potential role of government policy in ending this persistent scandal of hungry people in an increasingly prosperous world. The discussion on each individual dimension of food and nutrition security identified alternative, feasible and potentially successful interventions. In this final chapter, we focused in particular on those interventions that could simultaneously address the problems arising under more than one dimension to provide an efficient and effective strategy for ensuring the end of hunger and successfully contributing to a number of the recently announced Sustainable Development Goals and their related targets.

Note

1 While this goal has not been achieved at the aggregate level, it has been achieved in 72 of the 129 countries that have been monitored, 29 of which have also achieved the more ambitious World Food Summit Goal.

References

FAO. 2008. *An Introduction to the Basic Concepts of Food Security*. Rome: EC-FAO Food Security Programme.

FAO, IFAD and WFP. 2015. *The State of Food Insecurity in the World: Meeting the 2015 International Hunger Targets: Taking Stock of Uneven Progress*. Rome: FAO.

General Assembly on Sustainable Development Goals. 2014. *Open Working Group Proposal for Sustainable Development Goals*. New York: United Nations.

Shoaf Kozak, R., Lombe, M. and Miller, K. 2012. Global Poverty and Hunger: An Assessment of Millennium Development Goal #1. *Journal of Poverty*, 16, 469–485.

United Nations. 2014. *The Millennium Development Goals Report 2014*. New York: United Nations

United Nations Research Institute for Social Development. 2016. Policy Innovations for Transformative Change: Implementing the 2030 Agenda for Sustainable Development. *UNRISD Flagship Report 2016*. Geneva: United Nations Research Institute for Social Development.

World Food Summit. 1996. *Rome Declaration on World Food Security and World Food Summit Plan of Action*. Rome: World Food Summit.

2　Food security and hunger

Introduction

Many authors suggest that humans have an in-built sense of obligation to ensure that all people have sufficient food. Simone Weil (2002) points to this as an innate characteristic of human conscience that has not varied over millennia. She suggests that even the ancient Egyptians felt a deep sense of obligation to be in a position to say that they had never allowed any of their countrymen suffer from hunger. The early Christians were also very clear about this, and there are numerous quotes in the New Testament that emphasise that feeding the hungry is a fundamental duty of all individuals in society. In fact, all major faith groups, including Muslims, Christians, Jews and Hindus, can find clear guidance in their holy books and in their traditions, calling for strong action to fight hunger and poverty. And there are contemporary echoes of this approach in Maslow's (1987) hierarchy of needs that identifies food as one of the most fundamental needs at the very base of the hierarchy. More recently, these ideas have been discussed and summarised by Hulme (2015) in the context of motivating concerns about global poverty.[1] The most common motivation arises from people's desire to relieve the suffering of others, reflecting the idea that those who have secure access to food and other necessities should help those who do not have such access, even if they are not members of the same family or kinship group (Singer, 1972). A second set of arguments suggests that those who can meet their basic needs should help those who cannot, in order to promote social cohesion and reduce the likelihood that excluded and disadvantaged groups may threaten economic and social stability for everybody else. A final motivation is based on the idea that the economic and political structures that create and maintain current levels of global prosperity are also responsible for creating global hunger and poverty. Thus, citizens in industrialised countries with mature political and economic systems have a duty to confront the problems of global poverty and hunger, since these problems are a side effect of the political, economic and financial systems supporting their prosperity.

The efforts of individuals and societies to discharge this duty to the poor and hungry have taken many forms over the centuries, and the ongoing failure of these efforts has called into question not only the global food production system, but also the economic and political processes through which resources are allocated between individuals and groups in society. Our interest here and throughout this book is in economic aspects of this problem.

This chapter focuses on how our definition of hunger, our understanding of how it comes about and our approaches to how it is measured have evolved in recent decades. Above all, this chapter is about the human story of hunger, those who are hungry, why, where and when.

In the next section, we consider alternative definitions of hunger and the lack of food security and discuss current understanding of these concepts. We focus in particular on how the four 'dimensions' of food security guide policy makers towards specific aspects of the hunger problem and consider a number of alternative approaches to food security measurement.

This sets to scene for a discussion, in the third section, of the current situation and recent trends in the extent and prevalence of hunger around the world. We also consider the data on which this analysis is based and the underlying data limitations, before reviewing some recent projections of food demand and supply to 2050. The final section summarises and concludes the discussion.

Hunger, food security and measurement

The Oxford English Dictionary defines hunger as "the uneasy or painful sensation caused by want of food . . . the exhausted condition caused by want of food". But the truly insidious nature of hunger is better illustrated by the following quotation:

> For hunger is a curious thing: at first it is with you all the time, waking and sleeping and in your dreams, and your belly cries out insistently, and there is a gnawing and a pain as if your very vitals were being devoured, and you must stop it at any cost, and you buy a moment's respite even while you know and fear the sequel. Then the pain is no longer sharp but dull, and this too is with you always, so that you think of food many times a day and each time a terrible sickness assails you, and because you know this you try to avoid the thought, but you cannot, it is with you. Then that too is gone, all pain, all desire, only a great emptiness is left, like the sky, like a well in drought, and it is now that the strength drains from your limbs, and you try to rise and find that you cannot, or to swallow water and your throat is powerless, and both the swallow and the effort of retaining the liquid taxes you to the uttermost.
>
> (Markandaya, 2002)

Food security and hunger

When it comes to operational definitions, it is important to distinguish between those that are focused on identifying acute episodes of hunger arising because of physical, biological or political emergencies (often the result of war, conflict or natural disasters), and those that identify chronic longer term problems.

Acute episodic hunger, like the conflict and natural disasters that typically give rise to it, is mostly location-specific and is generally indicated by displacement of people where individuals and families move away from affected locations to seek refuge in other areas. In these circumstances, we can say that hunger is self-revealed by the actions of those who move in response to the lack of food. Hunger relief activities and the need to establish 'collection points' are a direct response to the emergence of this type of hunger. Targeting of relief activities is not generally a major issue in these circumstances.

Chronic hunger is much more difficult to identify and measure, since people generally do not directly admit to being victims. This has become a major concern of the Food and Agricultural Organisation of the United Nations (FAO) and is now a focus of a major annual report on the State of Food Insecurity around the world.

One convenient starting point is to consider definitions of food security, for example that initially promulgated by the World Food Summit (1996) and updated by FAO et al. (2015); viz. "Food security exists when all people, at all times, have physical, social and economic access to sufficient, safe and nutritious food that meets their dietary needs and food preferences for an active and healthy life".

This definition pointed to a multi-faceted view of food security that focused first of all on the physical availability of food, the 'food first' approach that dominated policy discussions and policymaker thinking through the 1950s to 1970s (Shaw, 2007). This approach was encouraged by the unarguable success of the Green Revolution (Pingali, 2012) in making more food available to feed the hungry, and prompted widespread debates about providing sufficient resources for agricultural research, extension and investment in farm modernisation, as well as discussions about the establishment of international food reserves.

However, it was already becoming clear that food availability on its own, though undeniably necessary, was not sufficient for elimination of hunger. In fact studies by Sen (1980, 1981) identified many situations where hunger and famine had serious human consequences even where and when there was more than sufficient food to provide an adequate diet for everybody. What Sen argued was that in addition to having sufficient food available, it was also necessary to ensure that those who needed food were able to purchase it at the ruling prices. He spoke about the exchange entitlements (Sen, 1981) of those who needed food and drew attention to the fact that famines were inevitably the result of poverty and not just food scarcity.[2]

This definition recognises four parallel food security dimensions: food availability, access to food, food utilisation and stability over time. Food availability (and its relationship to food needs) draws attention both to food production, the historical focus of food security discussions and also to food consumption driven by underlying changes in population, affluence and diet. The second dimension predominantly concerns economic access and the affordability of food. This focuses attention on the livelihoods of individuals and on the way in which these are influenced by agricultural production (for the rural poor), and by broader economic conditions, including food prices and policies for social safety nets and poverty alleviation.

Food utilisation, the third dimension, directs attention to how well people use the food that is available and to which they have access, in providing adequate nutrition. Here the focus is on satisfactory food preparation facilities and capabilities, including access to clean water and having sufficient knowledge to implement good nutritional practices as well as good hygiene. Important issues discussed in relation to this dimension of food security include those related to micronutrient availability (so-called hidden hunger), those related to dietary change and obesity, those related to intra-household food allocation, and those related to food waste. The fourth dimension of food security considers the need for stability, sustainability and resilience, in relation to food availability, food affordability and food utilisation.

Approaches to measuring food security

Maxwell (1996) has pointed out the many ways in which thinking about food security has evolved over recent decades. He echoes the shift from a 'food first' approach that maintains a focus on food availability, to focusing on affordability and livelihoods discussed in previous paragraphs. At the same time, he sees a parallel shift from a focus on measuring food security at global and national levels to establishing measurements at individual level. Finally, he sees a shift from the use of objective measures of food availability and nutrition outcomes to indicators based on subjective assessment of individual attitudes.

While the paradigm shift envisaged by Maxwell may be clear-cut and may not yet have fully taken place, the influence of this shift on thinking about food security has been profound. As a result, several measures of food security are currently in use. For example, the FAO now routinely provides a number of indicators for each dimension of food security: five indicators for food availability, nine for food affordability and access, ten for food utilisation and nutritional outcomes and seven for stability (FAO et al., 2014).[3]

Prevalence of Undernourishment (PoU) *Index:* In addition to these measures, the principal interest here is the most often quoted summary measure of overall food security, the Prevalence of Undernourishment Index. In this context, undernourishment and hunger refer to the continued inability of households and individuals to consume sufficient food to provide the energy required to carry on a healthy and active life. Sufficient food in this case is measured with reference to a consumption benchmark established by nutritionists; a person is considered undernourished if their regular intake of energy is considered by nutritionists to be below that required to cover the minimum requirements for a sedentary lifestyle (FAO et al., 2012). The FAO measure also requires that the individual's energy consumption be below the benchmark level for a full year before they are considered undernourished. In this way, the FAO Prevalence of Undernourishment indicator measures a clearly and narrowly defined concept of undernourishment that focuses specifically on energy deprivation over a complete year. It does not consider other aspects of hunger and undernutrition, such as the shorter-term effects of temporary food crises, the inadequate intake of other essential nutrients, such as protein, vitamins and minerals, or the effects of any costs or sacrifices incurred as individuals and households struggle to maintain their energy consumption levels.

The starting point for determining estimates of this indicator is the preparation of national food balance sheets. Historically, these balance sheets represent the first systematic attempt to measure the food security situation, introduced more than 100 years ago (FAO, 2001). Since then, the methodology has been refined and extended and now covers most countries in the world. For each country, a food balance sheet provides an estimate of the amount of food from each primary commodity that is available for human consumption during a specified period. This will include the amount produced, the quantity imported and any change in stocks that may have occurred. This gives the supply available during that period. After making adjustments for quantities exported, amounts fed to livestock and used for seed, and amounts lost during storage and transportation, the food balance sheet provides an estimate of supplies available for human consumption.

Though it provides a basic parameter in judging national food security on its own, the lack of detail in a food balance sheet is its major drawback. One particular problem is that food balance sheets in recent years have provided a positive measure of food security (indicating a complete absence of food insecurity) across all continents and most countries. At the same time, it is clear from other information that many people are still hungry, even in countries and regions with a positive food balance, so there has been significant motivation to explore alternative approaches to measuring food security.

One approach that has been adopted by the FAO, and recently rolled out for all countries, is based on modelling the distribution of food consumption across individuals in each country and region (FAO et al., 2012). This involves a multi-step procedure. The first step is choosing a suitable mathematical form for the distribution. Secondly, detailed information about individual or household food consumption (usually derived from expenditure survey data in combination with price data) is used to provide estimates of the relevant distribution parameters (for example mean, variance, skewness). As the penultimate step, the complete distribution is calculated for a given country or region, once the necessary parameters are estimated. Finally, a suitable cut-off point is chosen (related to the nutritional requirements of individuals in this country or region), and the number of people who are consuming below this level as a percentage of total population provides the relevant estimate of the prevalence of undernourishment.

This approach has the twin advantages of making good use of limited available data and being capable of providing estimates for any areas in which suitable data can be provided. This is now a widely used approach despite the many criticisms arising from assumptions about the form of the distribution, the computation of distributional parameters, and significant controversy about a suitable cut-off point in a wide range of circumstances. Furthermore, this approach remains dependent on having data from household food consumption surveys.

Household food consumption surveys provide the ultimate data set for food security analysis both in terms of level of detail and in terms of the level of quality control exercised. However, they are more expensive and time consuming compared to the food balance sheet approach. Nevertheless, they have one major advantage: the information collection procedure can be integrated with more general household expenditure surveys, and these are an essential policy maker's tool for economic policy design, implementation and monitoring. This means that food expenditures and food prices are collected in the context of an overall survey of household expenditure, enhancing data quality by providing a range of checks on the data collected.

However, one significant drawback of all the approaches discussed so far is that they focus on food consumption or food available for consumption, and do not explicitly consider actual nutritional outcomes. They allow us to determine that a specific proportion of a given population is consuming less food than they need according to the chosen cut-off criterion. They do not provide information about a range of other important characteristics. For example, they do not measure the potential impairment of the biological, social or economic performance of these people or allow the assessment of the extent to which recovery might be possible. In addition, they provide no information about what interventions might be required to enhance resilience and improve the chances of recovery. Some of this information is available only from anthropometric surveys that set out to measure the extent to which a given population (usually children under five) have failed to develop according to established norms for the country, region or group. These surveys (CRS, 1998; WHO, 2010) are often undertaken by medically trained people and are therefore much more expensive than other approaches. For this reason, and because of the detailed planning needed, the results of these surveys provide rather sparse and intermittent coverage of groups that are vulnerable to chronic hunger.[4] Results from these surveys are often presented for large aggregate groups, but measures for individual countries or groups within countries are not yet systematically available.

Global Hunger Index(GHI)*:* One remaining problem with the measures discussed so far is that, individually, they focus only on a single aspect of hunger. While the multi-faceted nature of hunger can be considered informally, for example by reviewing some or all of the suite of indicators prepared by FAO, the Global Hunger Index (GHI) (von Grebmer et al., 2015) provides a single indicator that represents an aggregate of a number of these dimensions. This index is based on a weighted average of four different indicators. General undernourishment arising from the under-supply of food is represented by the proportion of people that are undernourished (weighted 1/3) – this is the index of food insecurity already discussed above. Two indicators of child under-nutrition are used, wasting (low weight for height) and stunting (low height for age), each weighted 1/6. The fourth indicator is the under-five child mortality rate, also weighted 1/3(Weismann et al., 2015); each indicator is standardised before weighting to account for differences in the units of measurement.

Current situation and trends

Extent and prevalence of hunger

According to the FAO and the World Food Programme, 795 million people were suffering from hunger in 2015 (FAO et al., 2015). This is the estimated number of people across all countries who suffered continued inability to consume sufficient food to provide the minimum amount of energy required to support a life of minimal physical activity over a full year, i.e. the Prevalence of Undernourishment indicator discussed above. As already pointed out, this measure considers only chronic hunger, ignoring any short-term or temporary food shortages, including seasonal hunger and 'hungry gap' (end-of-season) shortages. More importantly, it considers only calorie consumption and ignores any deficiencies in other nutrients. These calculations also ignore any attempts by individuals and families to cope with the food deficit, which may include livestock slaughter and the sale of productive assets, such as tools, machinery etc., that would seriously compromise future food security.

Figure 2.1 illustrates how these hungry people are distributed across regions and countries. Southern Asia accounts for 36 per cent of these people, around 281 million, while 28 per cent or 218 million are in Sub-Saharan Africa, and 18 per cent (145 million) are in Eastern Asia. South-Eastern Asia, North Africa and Western Asia, and Latin America and the Caribbean account for 15 per cent of the remaining 18 per cent.

Key details behind these numbers are illustrated in Figure 2.2, which presents the numbers of undernourished people in Sub-Saharan Africa, in Eastern Asia, in Southern Asia and in South-Eastern Asia, as well as the numbers in Developing

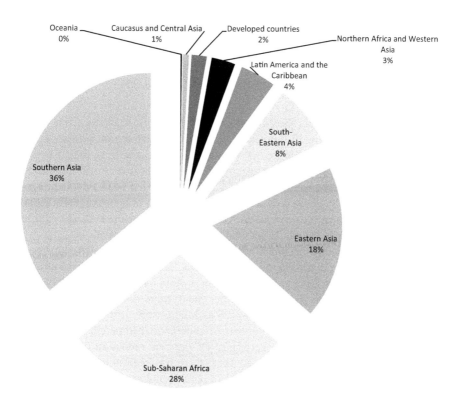

Figure 2.1 Undernourishment in 2014–16 by region

Source: Based on data from Table A.2 FAO Food Security Indicators, FAOSTAT, February 2016

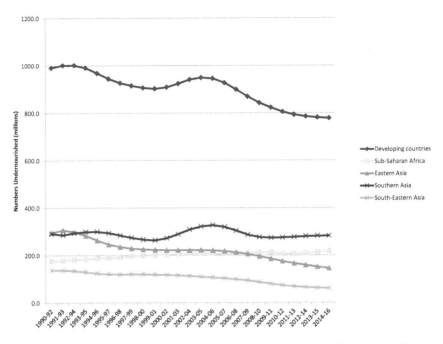

Figure 2.2 Numbers of undernourished people 1990–92 to 2014–16 by region (millions)

Source: FAO Food Security Indicators Table A.2, FAOSTAT, February 2016

Countries as a whole, over the 24-year period 1990–92 to 2014–16. Correspond-ing information, showing the percentage of people in each region who are under-nourished, is presented in Figure 2.3. For all developing countries, there has been a slight increase in numbers at the start of the period to just over one billion under-nourished people in the run-up to the mid-1990s. There has been a decline to just under 778 million by the end of the period, a reduction of approximately 22 per cent. At the same time, the percentage of undernourished people in these countries (Figure 2.3) fell from around 23 per cent to just under 13 per cent.

However, the picture becomes more complex when the detailed changes in individual regions are considered. For example, the number of undernourished people in both South-Eastern Asia and Eastern Asia has declined steadily from 1990–92. For Southern Asia, on the other hand, there have been more mixed fortunes; numbers increase until 1994–96 and there were further increases from 1999–01 until 2004–06. In fact, numbers of undernourished people in this region fell only to 281 million by 2014–16, just a 3 per cent reduction from 1990–92 levels. For Sub-Saharan Africa in contrast, there has been a steady increase in numbers in most years, giving an overall 24 per cent increase from 176 million in 1990–92 to 218 million in 2014–16.

In the case of prevalence of undernourishment, as measured by the percent-age of population who are undernourished (Figure 2.3), there is a similarly com-plex picture. However, prevalence has declined not just for developing regions

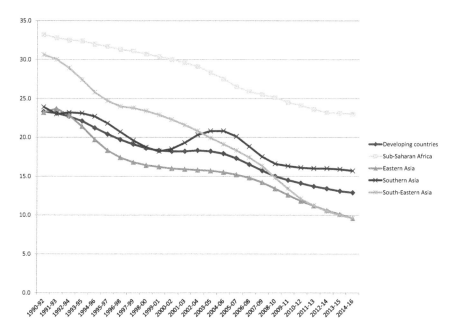

Figure 2.3 Percentage of people undernourished 1990–92 to 2014–16 (per cent)
Source: FAO Food Security Indicators Table 2.6, FAOSTAT, February 2016

as a whole, but for each of the individual regions examined here, including Sub-Saharan Africa. The decline has been continuous in Sub-Saharan Africa, in South-Eastern Asia and in Eastern Asia. However, in South Asia, there was a significant increase in the prevalence of undernourishment over the six-year period 2000–02 to 2006–08, and this is reflected in a slight upturn for developing countries as a whole in 2002–04.

The GHI scores in Table 2.1 are based on those presented in von Grebmer et al. (2015). Again, even with this more comprehensive multi-faceted measure, a similar overall picture emerges.

The data in Table 2.1 show significant progress since 1990, with the aggregate global value of the GHI declining from 35.4 to 21.7, a reduction of nearly 40 per cent. These numbers should be interpreted in the context where values of over 50.0 are regarded as extremely alarming, 35–49.9 as alarming, 20.0–34.9 as serious, 10–19.9 as moderate and less than 9.9 as low (International Food Policy Research Institute, 2015). On this scale, the hunger problems in South Asia and Sub-Saharan Africa in 2015 continue to be classified as serious, while those in all other regions are classified as moderate or low.

Data limitations

Ongoing chronic hunger is well documented, and these numbers will exclude many people caught up in more acute episodes of famine and hunger. The problem

Table 2.1   Global hunger index scores – selected years 1990 to 2015

Region	1990	1995	2000	2005	2015
Latin America and the Caribbean	19.0	17.0	13.7	10.9	8.0
Eastern Europe and Commonwealth of Independent States	-	15.1	14.1	10.2	8.3
Near East and North Africa	18.7	18.5	15.9	14.6	11.5
East and South-East Asia	28.6	26.8	20.6	18.1	13.2
South Asia	47.7	43.0	38.2	37.6	29.4
Sub-Saharan Africa	47.3	47.4	44.6	39.8	32.2
World	35.4	33.6	29.9	27.9	21.7

Source: Based on data from von Grebmer et al., 2015

is mainly a methodological one; chronic hunger can be identified from a distance, by distribution modelling, national household surveys and the like, whereas those who suffer acute problems of hunger can only be identified on a very personal face-to-face basis. For example, the United Nations World Food Programme, the body charged with responsibility for responding to acute food shortages, provides detailed information on ongoing operations but, as far as can be determined, does not provide aggregate historical information that can be analysed alongside the FAO's data on food insecurity. This persistent problem limits the analysis that can be undertaken.

It remains important to recognise the admitted limitations of the data on food insecurity and in particular to query any tendencies to over-state or under-state the extent of food insecurity in specific circumstances. The most widely used method for estimating numbers and prevalence of food insecurity and undernourishment starts with modelling the distribution of food expenditures among households. This estimated distribution of household expenditures is then used to calculate the number of people who are not consuming sufficient food to provide the kilocalories needed to support a lifestyle that involves some relatively small amount of physical activity in each specific country or region. Clearly, the values of the parameters used, to convert expenditures to food purchases and to convert food purchases to available energy, will have a significant influence on the outcome; in the absence of specific information to the contrary, there is no expectation of systematic bias here. The parameter specifying minimum daily requirements may also be subject to discussion and dispute, but, again, without expectation of systematic bias.

However, there is an in-built assumption in the remainder of the estimation procedure that the energy calculated to be available at household level is consumed pro-rata by all household members. This part of the procedure ignores two important processes that could have important ramifications for the food security of household members in specific circumstances.

In the first instance, this procedure ignores household food utilisation and the propensity of households to waste some proportion of the food available. The lack of modern storage facilities including refrigeration, the propensity for vicarious consumption of food by insects and pests and the over-zealous interpretation of use-by dates and other food safety information are important factors here. This will mean that the procedure will systematically overestimate the average level of energy consumption for a significant number of households and underestimate food insecurity and undernourishment.

In addition, the procedure takes no account of intra-household dynamics and resource allocation processes. A number of studies suggest that resource allocation among individual household members is almost never on an equal basis (Agarwal and Herring, 2013; Quisumbing and Smith, 2007). Male members engaged in physical work will generally have priority over women and children. This also means that the method used will tend to overestimate the number of people who are consuming sufficient food to meet the minimum energy standard. However, the method also ignores the distribution of activities among household members and the distribution between different households. Whereas the *intra*-household food allocation mechanism may well take into account the intra-household distribution of physical activity, the *inter*-household activity distribution is not properly accounted for using a fixed cut-off standard. Depending on the level at which the standard is set, it could result in either an over-estimation or an under-estimation of the number of people who are not consuming sufficient energy.

Svedberg (2002) also examined the FAO modelling approach in detail and concluded that there were systematic biases that could result in overestimation of the prevalence of undernutrition. Svedberg's thesis is that the FAO continue to use a mechanism that is systematically biased, partly because it ignores the way in which the calories required vary across a given population, focusing instead on a single 'cut-off' value representing the minimum calories required by an individual of average size and metabolism undertaking a minimum level of day-to-day activity. As already explained, this cut-off value is applied to an estimate of the distribution of available calories across the members of the population. In a stylised simulation, Svedberg compares the estimates obtained using this approach with those that would be obtained by an alternative method that takes account of the distribution of requirements across members of the population (arising from the variation in size, metabolism and physical activity); i.e. using a method based on a joint bivariate distribution (calories required and calories available) rather than a univariate distribution (just calories available). He shows that for a given set of parameter values, the new method based on the bivariate distribution provides estimates of the number of hungry and undernourished people that are systematically higher in comparison with those provided by the FAO's univariate cut-off point method. In other words, the widely used FAO approach systematically underestimates the prevalence of undernutrition in each country and region and across the globe. Svedberg also critically examines the parameter values used in the FAO methodology and goes on to show that these are not always well founded. He provides estimates of undernutrition that are systematically lower than those based on the FAO parameter values using what he describes as more acceptable parameter values. Thus, he asserts that the FAO approach tends to underestimate undernutrition due to using a biased methodology and at the same time tends to overestimate undernutrition due to choice of biased parameter values. Finally, he shows, using demonstrably reasonable parameter values, that the net effect of these opposing tendencies is a net overestimation of the prevalence of undernutrition.

Barrett (2010) argues that the estimates of undernutrition used for policy analysis, and the basis for these estimates, can have important effects on policy choice and implementation. For example, he suggests that estimates based on assessments of national food availability normally obtained using food balance sheets, focus attention on food aid shipments in the short term and on agricultural production strategies in the longer term. This is the 'food first' approach that has dominated thinking about food security for many decades. Only in the past quarter century has the impact of Sen's work begun to promote acknowledgement that lack of food access accounts for more food insecurity than lack of food availability. This has generated more interest in family-focused survey approaches and individual-focused anthropometric approaches to measurement of undernutrition and food insecurity, directing more attention to strategies for price stabilisation, poverty alleviation and social protection. He also emphasises that current approaches to measuring the prevalence of undernutrition are unavoidably backward looking and the most up-to-date estimates are usually many months out of date when available, so they do not provide information that can be used to predict the emergence of hunger problems or to direct actions to avoid or prevent these problems. In addition, most of these estimates refer to national food availability and do not refer to trans-national, intra-national or household/individual-level food problems arising from issues with availability, access or utilisation.

The other main problem with the FAO methodology is that it ignores the possibility of deficiencies in other essential nutrients. Since availability of these nutrients is closely but not perfectly correlated with availability of energy, a calorie-deficient diet will very likely also be deficient in these nutrients. However, there will also be circumstances when a calorie-sufficient diet will be deficient in these nutrients. Continuing research has identified a large number of these nutrients and the number continues to expand as further detailed research is being undertaken. As pointed out by Biesalski (2013), the principal nutrient deficiencies with the most serious potential consequences for child development and learning are iodine, vitamin A, iron and zinc. The visible clinical consequences of these deficiencies include blindness, anaemia, skin lesions and diarrhoea, goitre and cretinism. Ultimately, the consequences will include impaired development and learning for children and generally compromised performance, both mentally and physically, for adults. More importantly, the numbers of people potentially affected by this type of 'hidden hunger' is likely to exceed by a wide margin the numbers currently identified as suffering from a deficit in energy intake. It is at least arguable that the consequences of not taking action to remedy this problem are likely to be more serious than the consequences of chronic energy deficiency. See Chapter 5 for a further discussion of this problem.

Projected changes in food demand and supply to 2050

The continuing increase in the demand for food is well documented and relatively uncontroversial. For example a High Level Expert Forum convened by the Food and Agriculture Organisation (FAO, 2009) determined that this increase is being driven by population increase, urbanisation, increasing affluence (as increases in income encourage dietary changes) and economic growth that appears to be progressively eliminating the worst levels of absolute poverty across the world.

These and subsequent analyses point to an expected increase in population by about one third to over nine billion by 2050; this increase is concentrated in developing countries, with those in Sub-Saharan Africa growing fastest (around 114 per cent) and East and South-East Asia growing slowest, at around 13 per cent. At the same time, the proportion of population living in urban areas is expected to increase to about 72 per cent, rising from around 49 per cent at present. Rural population is projected to continue increasing for some time but numbers are expected to start declining from around 2020. Average per capita incomes will continue to increase, with incomes in developing countries continuing to outpace those in developed countries (FAO, 2009).[5]

An important impact of a growing and increasingly affluent population is an expansion in the demand for food, reflecting both the needs of the increased number of people and the increased ability of people to fulfil their felt needs for food consumption as less people find their demand for food constrained by income. In addition, higher incomes encourage a 'nutrition transition' (Popkin, 1993), where diets are shifted away from cereals and tubers and towards higher proportions of vegetables, meat and dairy products. This has particular implications for the demand for cereals, which increases in order to supply both the additional food for growing numbers who can now afford a full diet and the increased demand for animal feed to supply the additional amount of meat and dairy products now required by the more affluent population.

The asymmetric growth in income between developed countries and developing countries has other important implications. On the one hand, it will lead to a reduction in income differences between developed and developing countries, but on the other hand, it is not expected to reduce the already significant disparities between countries and regions in the developing world and may even exacerbate the already accelerating differences within both developed and developing countries.

Given these changes the demand for food is expected to continue increasing (Alexandratos and Bruinsma, 2012). The demand for cereals, for both human food and animal feed, is expected to increase, reaching around three billion tonnes per annum by 2050. At the same time, the demand for meat is expected to reach more than 450 million tonnes per annum.

The feasibility of producing this additional cereals, meat and dairy products, has been explored in a wide range of studies by FAO and other organisations.[6] In particular, these studies have considered the continued slowing in the rates of growth of the yields of the main cereals crops and the potential availability of land and water resources to support the additional production needed (FAO, 2009). Many studies have shown that the world has considerable reserves of cultivable land. However, much of these reserves cannot be converted to crop and livestock production (currently in other uses, or in remote areas lacking access and infrastructure), and arable land is being lost to degradation, salinisation and urban expansion. With this in mind, FAO has estimated that approximately 110 million hectares could be converted to agricultural use up to 2050, while approximately 40 million hectares are likely to be lost to degradation and urbanisation. This leaves a net gain of around 70 million hectares (Alexandratos and Bruinsma, 2012).

Discussion of these issues is taken up again in Chapter 3, concluding that the expected changes in productivity and resource availability would allow expansion in food production to meet projected increases in food requirements and demand.

Summary and conclusions

Concerns that all people have sufficient food pervade the thinking of major faith groups and more widely in society. These concerns may be motivated by a desire to relieve suffering among fellow humans or by a desire to promote social cohesions and reduce the likelihood of conflict that could damage our own welfare. Alternatively, there may be a sense of duty to confront the problems of global poverty and hunger created in part by the political, economic and financial systems supporting our prosperity. The focus here is on food insecurity and hunger as a reflection of the continuing failure of our collective and individual efforts to discharge this duty to the poor and hungry.

The intensely personal and potentially devastating effects of hunger are briefly considered as well as the conventional definition of food security that refers to the ability of individuals to command physical, social and economic access to sufficient safe and nutritious food that is consistent with dietary needs and food preferences and sustains an active and healthy lifestyle. This definition highlights the four dimensions of food security, availability, affordability, utilisation and stability, and provides the basic framework for subsequent chapters of this book.

Alternative approaches to measurement of food security and hunger are reviewed, emphasising the currently popular Prevalence of Undernourishment (PoU) indicator and considering the more recently developed multi-dimensional measure, the Global Hunger Index. The potential advantages that might be gained by adopting measures that are more firmly focused on the experience of individuals rather than on the overall distribution of dietary energy consumption are briefly investigated. Such measures might be more firmly based on household consumption or expenditure surveys or on more detailed anthropometric measurements of body size and weight for samples of adults and children.

The current global extent and prevalence of undernutrition is briefly considered. Here the data call attention to the wide variation in experiences between different countries and regions across the globe. Over 60 per cent of people who suffer chronic hunger are based in South Asia and Sub-Saharan Africa. At the same time, the numbers of hungry people across all developing countries has declined by around 22 per cent since the mid-1990s, while the prevalence of undernourishment in these countries has declined from 23 per cent to under 13 per cent of the population. Considering individual regions, the data indicate that prevalence of undernourishment has declined for all regions of the world, including Sub-Saharan Africa, since 1990–92. However, over that time span, the number of undernourished people has fallen by only around 3 per cent in South Asia, and numbers actually increased in Sub-Saharan Africa. This overall picture is confirmed by both the PoU index and the GHI index. Thus, the successful experiences in combating hunger across East and South-East Asia must be considered in the light of mixed experiences in South Asia and the less successful experiences in Sub-Saharan Africa.

However, the potential limitations of these measures must also be taken on board. For example, the starting point for the PoU indicator is the availability of food at a national level indicated in country-level food balance sheets. This food is assumed to be available for consumption by individual households and by individuals within households. This means that any losses due to household food waste or any adjustments in the allocation of food between members of the household are not considered. In addition, the measure of undernourishment is based on a single, broad-based food requirement without considering differences in food requirements across members of the population due to differences in body size, levels of activity etc. It has been shown that these problems result in inaccurate and systematically biased measures of undernourishment. Two other problems have been identified with these measures: they are focused on what has happened in the past and are of no use in predicting the emergence of hunger and nutrition problems, and they deal only with energy consumption and so completely ignore undernutrition problems that can arise because of deficiencies in vitamins, minerals or other nutrients. However, the PoU indicator remains the measure of choice, since it is the lowest-cost and most widely available measure. Nevertheless, the advantages remain for measures that consider more than one aspect of food security or are more firmly focused on household and individual consumption and nutritional outcomes, so use of these measures is likely to increase.

To round off the discussion in this chapter and anticipating more detailed discussion and analysis in Chapter 3, we briefly review projected changes in food supply and demand. Changes in population, income and urbanisation represent the main factors that lead both to a direct increase in the overall demand for food as well as to changes in dietary composition via the nutrition transition, with reduced proportions of starchy cereals and tubers and increased proportions of vegetables, meat and dairy products. These dietary changes lead to a further indirect effect on food demand to include the additional cereals needed as feed for the livestock supplying additional meat and dairy products. The overall impact amounts to an annual increase of around three billion tonnes of cereals and over 450 million tonnes of meat by 2050. As pointed out in Chapter 3, anticipated changes in availability and productivity of land, water and other resources are likely sufficient to ensure that supplies expand to meet these additional demands.

Notes

1 Hulme points out the close and sometimes overlapping relationship between the concepts of poverty and hunger. He suggests that, in a simplified framework, poverty can be seen as 'lack of food'. This is reflected in the widespread practice of defining 'extreme poverty' in terms of the ability to access a minimum level of dietary energy needed for survival and reproduction (generally assumed to be around 2,300 calories per day for an 'average' adult) and is consistent with the very general notion that poverty involves "lacking the means to procure the necessities of life".
2 Chapter 4 provides a more detailed discussion and analysis of these ideas.
3 For a complete list of these indicators, see Table A2.1 in Annex 2, FAO et al., 2014
4 Information provided by these surveys includes: (a) birth weights of children born under 2.5 kg; (b) proportion of underweight children (those who are more than two or three standard deviations below median weights for the given age group); (c) prevalence of wasting (those who are more than two or three standard deviations below median weight for given height group); and (d) prevalence of stunting (those who are more than two or three standard deviations below median height for given age group).
5 A more detailed analysis of these trends is presented in Chapter 3.
6 See Chapter 3 for a brief summary of these analyses.

References

Agarwal, B. and Herring, R. 2013. Food Security, Productivity and Gender Inequality. *In:* Herring, R. J. (ed.) *The Oxford Handbook of Food, Politics and Society.* New York: Oxford University Press.

Alexandratos, N. and Bruinsma, J. 2012. *World Agriculture Towards 2030/2050: The 2012 Revision.* Rome: FAO.

Barrett, C. B. 2010. Measuring Food Insecurity. *Science*, 327, 825–828.

Biesalski, H. K. 2013. *Hidden Hunger.* Berlin: Springer-Verlag.

CRS. 1998. *Anthropometric Survey Manual.* Baltimore, MD: Catholic Relief Services.

FAO. 2001. *Food Balance Sheets – A Handbook.* Rome: FAO.

FAO. 2009. *High Level Expert Forum – How to Feed the World in 2050* [Online]. Rome: FAO. Available: www.fao.org/fileadmin/templates/wsfs/docs/expert_paper/How_to_Feed_the_World_in_2050.pdf [Accessed September 27 2016].

FAO, IFAD and WFP. 2012. *The State of Food Insecurity in the World: Economic Growth Is Necessary But Not Sufficient to Accelerate Reduction of Hunger and Malnutrition.* Rome: FAO.

FAO, IFAD and WFP. 2014. *The State of Food Insecurity in the World 2014: Strengthening the Enabling Environment for Food Security and Nutrition.* Rome: FAO.

FAO, IFAD and WFP. 2015. *The State of Food Insecurity in the World: Meeting the 2015 International Hunger Targets: Taking Stock of Uneven Progress.* Rome: FAO.

Hulme, D. 2015. *Global Poverty.* London: Routledge.

International Food Policy Research Institute. 2015. *Methodology: Calculation of the Global Hunger Index (GHI) Scores* [Online]. Washington, DC: IFPRI. Available: http://ghi.ifpri.org/methodology/ [Accessed June 2016].

Markandaya, K. 2002. *Nectar in a Sieve.* New York: Signet Classics.

Maslow, A. H. 1987. *Motivation and Personality.* New York: Harper Collins.

Maxwell, S. 1996. Food Security: A Post-Modern Perspective. *Food Policy*, 21, 155–170.

Pingali, P. L. 2012. Green Revolution: Impacts, Limits and the Path Ahead. *Proceedings of the National Academy of Sciences*, 109, 12302–12308.

Popkin, B. M. 1993. Nutritional Patterns and Transitions. *Population and Development Review*, 19, 138–157.

Quisumbing, A. and Smith, L. 2007. Intrahousehold Allocation, Gender Relations and Food Security in Developing Countries. *In:* Pinstrup-Anderson, P. and Cheng, F. (eds.) *Food Policy for Developing Countries: Case Studies*. Ithaca, NY: Cornell University.

Sen, A. 1980. Famines. *World Development*, 8, 613–621.

Sen, A. 1981. *Poverty and Famines: An Essay on Entitlement and Deprivation*. Oxford: Clarendon Press.

Shaw, D. J. 2007. *World Food Security: A History Since 1945*. New York: Palgrave Macmillan.

Singer, P. 1972. Famine, Affluence, and Morality. *Philosophy and Public Affairs*, 1, 231–232.

Svedberg, P. 2002. Undernutrition Overestimated. *Economic Development and Cultural Change*, 51, 5–36.

Von Grebmer, K., Bernstein, J., De Waal, A., Prasai, N., Yin, S. and Yohannes, Y. 2015. *Global Hunger Index: Armed Conflict and the Challenge of Hunger*. Bonn, Washington, DC and Dublin: Welthungerhilfe, International Food Policy Research Institute (IFPRI), and Concern Worldwide.

Weil, S. 2002. *The Need for Roots: Prelude to a Declaration of Duties Towards Mankind*. London: Routledge Classics.

Weismann, D., Biesalski, H-K., Von Grebmer, K. and Bernstein, J. 2015. Methodological Review and Revision of the Global Hunger Index (GHI). *ZEF Working Paper 139*. Bonn: Zentrum für Entwicklungsforschung (Center for Development Research).

WHO. 2010. *Nutrition Landscape Information System (NLIS) Country Profile Indicators – Interpretation Guide*. Geneva: World Health Organisation.

World Food Summit. 1996. *Rome Declaration on World Food Security and World Food Summit Plan of Action*. Rome: World Food Summit.

3 Food availability, food requirements and food production

Introduction

In this chapter, we discuss food availability, the first dimension of food security. As Sen (1981) pointed out, food availability is about the *existence* of sufficient food for people to eat, rather than every individual actually *having* enough food to eat. From this point of view, the adequacy of food availability is about the balance between food requirements and food production and not just about food production on its own. Here, we focus on issues related to this balancing process.

It is important to emphasise that even if food production is not the only determinant of food security, it remains a primary pillar of the whole food security edifice. Moreover, even if we can point to the outstanding performance of the global food production system over recent decades, there remain two problems.

Firstly, rates of production on currently used arable land will not provide adequate food and nutrition for the larger more affluent population that is projected for the latter half of the 21st century (Beddington et al., 2011). There are a number of carefully documented accounts of what increases in food production will be needed as these changes unfold, and these are summarised here.

Secondly, producing this additional food will impose additional demands on already limited and overstretched supplies of our basic resources, land and water. More importantly, if these resources are to prove adequate for the levels of production being demanded, crop yields and animal productivity will need to increase. In addition, while yield and productivity increases have been a dominant characteristic of the Green Revolution that has provided increased food security over past decades, there is strong evidence that these increases are faltering. This raises fundamental questions about whether the combined effect of changes in yield, productivity and resources will allow the increased levels of food production required, and whether current institutional constraints and incentives will promote the allocation of these resources to food production activities.

The next section of this chapter, therefore, examines how food requirements have evolved over recent decades and highlights the extent to which they are being driven by changes in population, urbanisation and incomes. The implications of these changes for transforming traditional diets (the nutrition transition) and for how this transition will influence food requirements are particularly important. Expected changes over the next decades are also explored.

In the third section, our attention switches to the other side of the food security balance, to production. Here we consider trends in crop yields and animal productivity, and how these may be affected by potential changes in the availability of land, water and irrigation infrastructure, as well as by the potential future availability of fertilisers and crop protection chemicals and by the development of more productive strains of plants and animals.

The fourth section considers the implications of these changes for crop and livestock production in developed and developing countries up to 2050 and includes an assessment of the potential impact of climate change on these production estimates. The fifth section provides a brief review of the impact on food availability of increased openness to trade, and the final section provides a summary of the issues discussed in this chapter and concludes with a discussion of potential interventions.

Food requirements: population, affluence, urbanisation and the nutrition transition

A wide range of studies that estimate future global food requirements and food production capacity have been undertaken in recent years and these are the principal sources of information used here. A typology of these studies, proposed by Reilly and Willenbockel (2010), distinguishes three main groups of studies; projections, exploratory scenarios and normative scenarios.

Projections focus on estimating future outcomes of the agricultural production system under a set of assumptions representing "business as usual" (so-called baseline scenarios), or focus on how the system might behave under a set of assumptions representing specific "what-if" scenarios. The study referred to in Chapter 2 (Alexandratos and Bruinsma, 2012) is the most-quoted example of this type of study. Other examples include McIntyre et al. (2009) investigating the impact of agricultural knowledge, science and technology on food security and sustainable development, and the study by Erb et al. (2009) that explores the implications of various combinations of land-use change and dietary change, and goes on to suggest that a global switch to the current Western "high meat" diet is not a feasible scenario.

Exploratory scenarios take a broader approach and investigate possible futures that may entail changes in the structure of the system (for example, a switch to organic agriculture) and its boundary conditions (for example, a reduction in the amount of arable land available). The best-known example of this type of study that focuses on world agricultural production is the Millenium Ecosystem Assessment (2005).

Normative scenarios have a more limited focus and are generally undertaken to establish alternative approaches to achieving pre-specified targets. The AGRIMONDE foresight study (Paillard et al., 2014) is an important example of this type of study that focuses on exploring the implications for feeding the world in 2050, of reduced inequality in food consumption and more sustainable agricultural production. An additional example is the UK Foresight Report (Beddington et al., 2011). This study also used 2050 as a target date and set out to make a case for reform of the global food system by highlighting the competing pressures of increasing demands for food in the context of limited changes in resources and productivity.

All these studies emphasise that there are a several feasible pathways for feeding the expected global population, and some of these are explored in this chapter. Much of the discussion here is based on Alexandratos and Bruinsma (2012). This study sets out to make statements about future demand for food (and future production of individual food commodities and groups of commodities), for individual countries, groups of countries and regions using data and expertise from a range of sources. Prior to publication, the resulting forecasts were reviewed in detail by experts and benefitted from specialist expertise on the particular circumstances surrounding production and marketing for individual commodities in individual countries and regions.

Most scientists and commentators agree that changes in population and changes in incomes are the main factors that have influenced global food requirements over recent decades and this influence continues into the future. In addition, the substantial increase in the percentage of the global population living in urban areas has contributed, alongside increasing affluence and the spread of 'Western' culture, to changes in the composition of diets.

Population

Table 3.1 presents the United Nations estimates of global populations for 1950 to 2015 and projections to 2100, confirming both the exponential growth that has been experienced in recent decades and the uncertainty about future rates of growth. In fact, the estimated mid-2015 world population of 7.4 billion is projected to increase by just over one billion reaching 8.5 billion in 2030. According to the 'medium fertility' projection (that assumes reduced fertility in those countries where family size is currently large and some increase where fertility is currently below replacement rate), the population is expected to reach 9.7 billion by 2050 and 11.2 billion by 2100. The study stresses that small variations in fertility can make significant difference. For example, the 'high fertility' projection assumes an extra half child per woman, leading to projected 10.8 billion in 2050 and 16.6 billion in 2100. By contrast, the 'low fertility' projection is based on half child per woman less than the medium fertility projection, leading to a

Table 3.1 Total global population (billions); estimates 1950–2010, projections to 2100

1950	1960	2000	2010	2015	2030	2050	2100
2.53	3.02	6.13	6.93	7.35	8.50[1]	9.73[1]	11.21[1]
					8.18[2]	8.71[2]	7.29[2]
					8.82[3]	10.80[3]	16.58[3]

Source: United Nations, *World population Prospects: The 2015 Revision*

1 'Medium' fertility change assumptions;
2 'Low' fertility change assumptions;
3 'High' fertility change assumptions

peak population of around 8.7 billion in 2050 and declining to 7.3 billion by 2100. Figure 3.1 presents these projections.

Focusing on the medium fertility projection, the report also points out that the majority of the additional 3.8 billion people in 2100 will be in developing countries. Populations in these countries are projected to increase from the current level of around 6.1 billion to 8.4 billion in 2050 and 9.9 billion in 2100, rising to around 89 per cent of total global population, from 83 per cent currently.

These numbers are derived by assuming that population growth rates decline significantly in the future, as illustrated in Figure 3.2. This reflects a trend that has been apparent since around 1990, such that five-year average annual growth rates decline from around 1.8 per cent per annum in the five-year periods 1980–85 and 1985–90 to just over 1.2 per cent per annum in 2000–05 and 2005–10. For the medium fertility projection, this declines to 0.87 per cent per annum in 2025–30, 0.57 per cent in 2045–50, and down to 0.13 per cent in 2095–2100. The corresponding figures for the low (and high) projection are 0.54 (1.17) per cent, 0.14 (0.98) per cent and −0.67 (0.79) per cent for 2025–30, 2045–50 and 2095–2100, respectively.

In all cases, however, it is important to emphasise that there remains substantial uncertainty surrounding these estimates, illustrated by the significant differences between the different projections even when there are only minimal changes in underlying fertility trajectories in the low, medium and high fertility scenarios. This uncertainty, and one of its key implications, is also emphasised by the way in which successive revisions to these numbers, undertaken by the United Nations

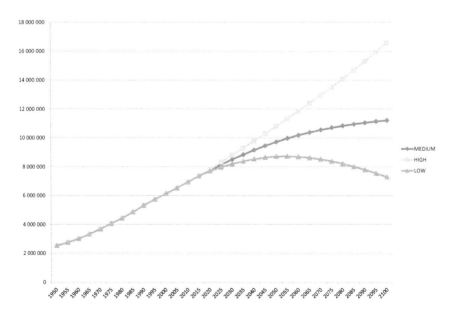

Figure 3.1 Global population (thousands); estimates 1950–2015; projections to 2100

Source: United Nations, World Population Prospects, 2015 Revision

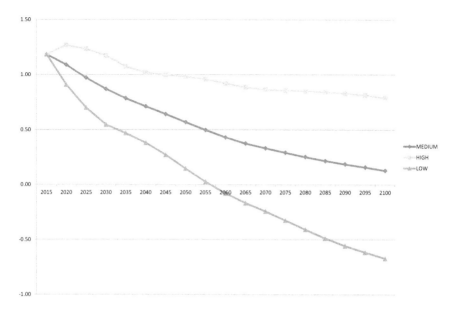

Figure 3.2 Assumed global population growth rates, 2015–2100

Source: United Nations, World Population Prospects, 2015 Revision

population division, lead to continuing increase in projected population levels. For example, world population projections for 2050 under the medium fertility assumption, have increased from 9.15 billion in the 2008 revision (United Nations, 2009), to 9.31 billion in the 2010 revision (United Nations, 2011), to 9.55 billion in the 2012 revision (United Nations, 2013) and to 9.73 billion in the 2015 revision (United Nations, 2015). It would appear that the main source of these revisions, and the main reason for the unrelenting increase in population projections, is due to continued upward revisions in the fertility estimates of populations in underdeveloped countries.

One further point is that, even as projected growth rates are continuing to decline, the annual increment in population is still quite substantial. For example, there were 83 million additional people each year in the decade ending in 2015, 70 million per year projected in the decade to 2035, remaining at a substantial 57 million each year as we approach 2050 (and this estimate has more than doubled from 27 million since the 2008 revision).

Another key point is that most of the growth in population is now confined to a small number of countries, either countries with high fertility (mainly in Sub-Saharan Africa), or countries with large populations (United Nations, 2015). In fact, half of the world's projected population growth during the period 2015 to 2050 will be in nine countries: India, Nigeria, Pakistan, the Democratic Republic of the Congo, Ethiopia, the United Republic of Tanzania, the United States of America, Indonesia and Uganda.

The 2015 study also highlights the persistence of high rates of population growth in a group of 48 countries designated as least developed, 27 of which are in Africa. Despite significantly reduced growth rates, these countries are expected to double their population from 2015 to 2050, reaching 1.9 billion and continuing to grow to around 3.2 billion by 2100. This tendency for population growth to remain concentrated in the poorest and least endowed countries and those with pre-existing food security problems, increases the urgency for finding solutions for the elimination of hunger and malnutrition. This difficulty is especially apparent when countries with large and rapidly growing rural populations remain heavily dependent on local resources and technology for the bulk of their food supplies and for employment and income that would enable them to purchase food from elsewhere.

There are a number of related issues here. First of all, there is a clear reminder of the views of Thomas Malthus (Malthus, 1798), who argued that population growth, and the consequent growth in food requirements, follows an exponential growth pattern. Because Malthus assumed that yields are fixed, food production can be increased only by bringing additional land into cultivation and is thus constrained to follow a linear growth pattern. This must mean that growth in food requirements must inevitably outstrip growth in food availability. Thus, population growth must be strictly managed in order to avoid widespread starvation. The historical record has demonstrated that the expansion in food availability has not been as constrained as he had assumed, due to accelerated growth in agricultural productivity in addition to expansion of the agricultural production base. In fact, Malthus himself had acknowledged this in later editions of his book. However, the spectre of global starvation due to a rapidly expanding population remained a popular theme even into the 1960s (Ehrlich, 1968), until eventually giving way to less alarming notions about the impact of population on biodiversity and the environment (Ehrlich and Ehrlich, 1992; Connelly, 2008).

Even with these changing views about the relationship between population, food availability and other economic activity, many commentators continue to insist that population growth and the levels of human fertility that underpin it restrict the growth of economic activity and the advancement of human wellbeing. These views are usually based on the simple arithmetic of sharing the fixed fruits of economic activity among an expanding number of individuals, an idea that is valid where people contribute only to consumption and have no impact on output. This argument has been widely disputed, and suggestions that additional people contribute to productivity as well as to consumption have come from a number of different sources.

For example, Boserup (1965) notes that in the Malthusian model, an inelastic food supply is the main factor governing the rate of population growth. This means that extraneous factors influencing changes in agricultural productivity determine the extent to which population can change at any given time. Boserup takes a contrarian approach that sees population growth as the driver, rather than the outcome, of agrarian change. In particular, she sees population growth as the main factor motivating the search for new farming techniques and influencing the decision to make the investments necessary to implement the newer more productive farming methods that are found. This provided a much more satisfactory explanation for the major increases in global population that were being experienced in the 1950s and the 1960s, rather than assuming that these were primarily driven by improvements in the conditions of food production – given that this was nearly a decade before the results of the "Green Revolution" were apparent.

Simon (1977, 1981, 1986) provides a more technical presentation of similar views that has proved much more controversial. He begins by pointing out that the Malthusian approach considers the impact of each additional person on an economy against a background of fixed levels of available capital resources and facilities for health, education and civic protection (fire, police etc.). In these circumstances, the dominant impact must be that of 'capital dilution', where taking on additional people must mean a reduction in the availability of capital and facilities for everybody. What Simon suggests is that, while each additional person will inevitably require resources from the economy, they will also reach a stage when they will contribute to these resources. These contributions will include additional labour and capital, but Simon focuses in particular on the contribution of each additional individual to the pool of ideas available to society, and ultimately to the advancement of technical knowledge and economic productivity, as these ideas are combined in a wide variety of ways. He emphasises that additional people, supported by an effective educational system, are likely to generate more ideas; and each additional idea added to the pool will lead to a significant increase in the number of possibilities for new combinations with other ideas, that could provide additional technical knowledge and enhanced productivity. Thus, the principal driver of technical change and economic growth is additional people; and in Simon's view, it made little difference whether these were the result of the birth of babies or of the arrival of immigrants, of population growth or immigration.

In terms of policy implications, a Malthusian mind set would support an argument for immediate and effective population control policies. In contrast, the approaches suggested by Boserup and Simon would suggest that the immediate costs of increased population be considered in balance with the longer term contribution of additional people to economic resources. They would stress in particular the contributions to incentives for technical change (Boserup) and/or the pool of ideas through which technical change is accomplished (Simon).

Affluence

Affluence is represented here by Gross Domestic Product (GDP) per capita. This is one widely quoted and readily available measure of the prosperity of countries and regions and of how prosperity changes over time. Here we show GDP per capita data for seven groups of countries covering the years 1992 to 2015 with projections to 2020. In an effort to account for differences in cost of living between countries, these estimates are presented on a Purchasing Power Parity (PPP) basis.

As illustrated in Figure 3.3, GDP per capita has consistently increased across all major regions of the world both for developed and developing countries, with two significant exceptions. In most developed countries, GDP per capita declined

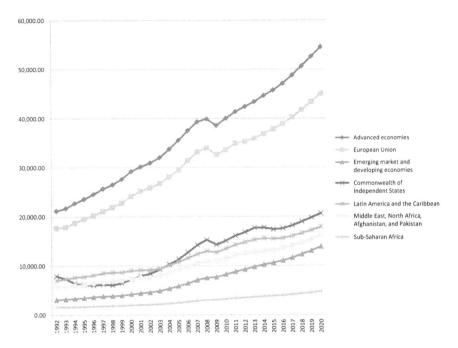

Figure 3.3 Gross domestic product per capita; Purchasing Power Parity basis, 1992–2020
Source: International Monetary Fund, World Economic Outlook Database, October 2015

sharply in 2009 but had recovered 2008 levels in all countries by 2011. Developing countries were mostly unaffected by this decline. The second major decline is in those countries of the former Soviet Union comprising the Commonwealth of Independent States where per capita GDP declined in 1993 and did not recover until 2002, as well as declining in 2009 and 2010. This data also shows that behind this general upward trend there remain four distinct groups of countries. At the top are the advanced economies that include the G7 countries and the European Union with per capita GDP ranging from around US$17,000 to over US$55,000 for the years examined. A second group of countries with per capita GDP that ranges between US$5,500 and US$21,000 over the same period includes countries in Latin America, the Commonwealth of Independent States and countries in the Middle East and North Africa as well as Afghanistan and Pakistan. A third group of countries, with per capita GDP in the range US$3,000 to US$14,000 are the Emerging market and developing economies. The fourth group of countries is in Sub-Saharan Africa with per capita GDP ranging from US$1,600 to just over US$4,500 over the same period. It is also interesting to note that, for the GDP data presented here, there is some evidence of divergence both between the four groups of countries presented here and even within some of the individual groups.

There is a two-fold impact of increasing affluence and incomes on food consumption. Firstly increasing affluence plays a central role in the alleviation of poverty and, as highlighted in Chapter 4, this improves individual access to food, contributing to the second pillar of food security, food accessibility and affordability. Secondly, increasing affluence is an important driver of dietary change and this is discussed in a later section of this chapter, on the nutrition transition.

Urbanisation

An additional characteristic of economic development in the 20th and 21st centuries is the increasing proportion of population living in urban areas and the corresponding decline in those available for rural economic activity including the production of food. These changes are illustrated in Figure 3.4 that shows the proportion of population living in urban areas from 1950, with projections to 2050, for countries aggregated by continent. Two groups are evident here. Europe, North America, Latin America and Australia/New Zealand show proportions urbanised ranging from just over 40 per cent for Latin America in 1950 to just over 90 per cent for Australia/New Zealand in 2050. By contrast, countries in Asia and Africa show proportions urbanised that vary from nearly 15 per cent (Africa in 1950) to around 65 per cent (Asia in 2050).

These changes represent a precipitous decline in farm numbers and are one important element of the so-called 'Farm Problem', another element is the low and unstable returns to labour and other resources used in agricultural production (Brandow, 1977). These changes are attributed to the interaction of a number of processes that have characterised the agricultural sector across most countries for most of the 19th and 20th centuries: restricted mobility of farm families, faced

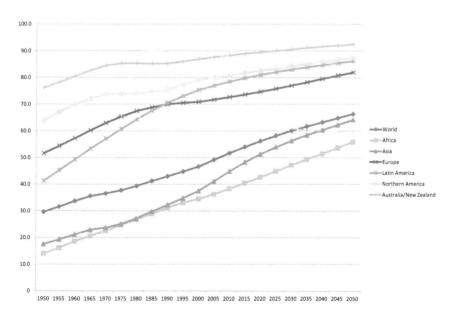

Figure 3.4 Per cent of population living in urban areas, 1950–2012 and projections to 2050

Source: UN Population Division, World Urbanisation Prospects, 2014 Revision

with inelastic supply and demand in agricultural markets, and continual techno-logical change leading to improvements in agricultural production techniques and the productivity of land and labour on farms (Sumner et al., 2010; Gardner, 1992).

There are important implications here for food requirements and availabil-ity. To begin with, off-farm migration and the resulting increase in urbanisation involves the migration of individuals and families from rural areas, where they have generally been making a contribution to the production of food both for their own consumption and, in most cases, also contributing to the marketable surplus. Since neither of these contributions continues following migration to urban areas, the demand for food in urban markets increases by the consumption needs of those who migrate, even as the supply of food to urban markets is potentially reduced by the shift of human resources to the urban labour pool.

It has also been noted that value added per worker is much higher in the non-agricultural sector than in agriculture in virtually all countries and especially in developing countries. This productivity gap between agriculture and other sectors of the economy is clearly visible in national accounts data of most countries and has been shown to persist even after a wide range of adjustments for potential errors in measuring working hours, worker quality and sector value added (Gollin et al., 2014). Hence, the movement of workers from rural areas to urban areas will almost certainly involve a net gain in overall productivity for the economy.

More importantly from our point of view, this movement of labour out of agri-culture is also associated with significant increases in agricultural productivity over many decades (Alston and Pardey, 2014). There is some agreement that this trend in the productivity of resources in agricultural production is likely to continue into the future (Fuglie, 2012). Further discussion of the alternative approaches to measuring productivity in agriculture and the extent to which growth in productiv-ity may be slowing down is in the section on "Resources, productivity and yields" later in this chapter.

The nutrition transition

An additional impact of both increased affluence and rural to urban migration concerns the type of food consumed, since affluence and urbanisation have been shown to significantly influence the nutrition transition that leads to increases in the consumption of meat and dairy products as these animal based food products replace the cereals, roots and tubers that had been dominant in more traditional rural diets.

This global transition, identified and documented by Popkin (1993), is an important process that underpins much of the observed changes in food consump-tion over recent decades. This has entailed a rapid increase in the consumption of meat, milk, eggs and vegetable oils, their increased importance as a source of calories, and their prominence in the diets of individuals in many countries across the globe. An important aspect of these changes is the emergence of prob-lems related to over-consumption of the resulting fat-enriched diet, leading to obesity and increased incidence of non-communicable diseases, such as diabetes and cardiac problems (Popkin, 2001; Popkin et al., 2012). While concern here is primarily with changes that influence the prevalence of under-nutrition rather than the extent of over-consumption, a more detailed consideration of problems related to obesity will be presented in Chapter 5.

As pointed out in Alexandratos and Bruinsma (2012), the nutrition transition is usually signalled by a rapid increase in the proportion of food calories consumed from sources related to livestock (based on meat, milk and eggs) and from vegetable oils. The dietary share of these food groups has risen from around 13 per cent to around 22 per cent in the decades since 1970, and this share is projected to exceed 25 per cent by 2030 and begin to approach 30 per cent by 2050. Nevertheless, cereals continue to be the dominant source of calories in developing countries and in the world as a whole with the global average just under 50 per cent. The current wide disparity between countries is illustrated by the observation that there are two large groups of countries where this proportion is as low as 20 per cent. Firstly, a group of developing countries where roots and tubers are the dominant source of calories (as for example in Rwanda, Burundi and Uganda). Secondly, high-income countries that have adopted a diet based on meat and livestock products. At the other extreme are countries where cereals provide up to 80 per cent of calories, those with rice-based diets (principally in Asia), and those (mainly African countries) where coarse grains are a principal source of calories.

Alexandratos and Bruinsma (2012) also point out that per capita direct use of cereals for food has been declining since the mid-1990s, both globally and for the developing countries as a group. This latter is occurring despite the fact that many countries in this group do not yet consistently provide sufficient food for all citizens and can be attributed to the changes in China and India, which tend to dominate observed aggregate changes in this group of countries, among which they account for nearly 50 per cent of population. If China and India are excluded, average per capita cereal use among the remaining developing countries has been increasing at a slow rate, the result of a balance between increases in consumption in some countries and reductions in others. While increases in per capita cereal consumption in this group of countries can be taken as an indicator of success in tackling food security issues, a reduction must be interpreted carefully. On the one hand, it may represent part of the evidence for dietary diversification to other products for many countries including China, the Republic of Korea, Turkey etc. On the other hand, this is not the case for all countries. In countries such as Zambia, the United Republic of Tanzania, the Democratic People's Republic of Korea, Yemen and a number of others, decline in cereals consumption per capita has been part of a broader failure in food security and is usually accompanied by a decline on overall per capita calorie intake.

In these circumstances, the net outcome for cereals consumption in developing countries is likely to involve an increase on current levels, arising from the net effect of a number of processes. First, there will be increases in cereals consumption in lower-income countries as diets adjust to overcome energy deficits and to diversify towards cereals consumption and away from the consumption of other staple products. This increase will be partially offset by a reduction in cereals consumption in countries with higher income levels, as part of a continued dietary diversification towards animal products. Total overall use of cereals, including use for seed, livestock feed, and industrial uses, such as for alcohol or starch production, is expected to increase.

Considering individual cereals, the reduction in per capita consumption is primarily driven by reduction in rice consumption across the high consuming developing countries; this reduction is offset only to a very limited extent by increases in per capita consumption, though still at relatively low levels, in developed countries. Wheat consumption per capita continues to rise in Sub-Saharan Africa, South Asia and Latin America, but this growth is offset by reductions in the remainder of the world. Coarse grain consumption for food has not been increasing in recent decades, remaining around 37 kg per person; yet this product category accounts for around 70 per cent of food consumption in many countries in Sub-Saharan Africa and over 40 per cent in Latin America. Maize is the predominant grain in most countries, though millet and sorghum are also important in some African countries. Industrial demand, particularly the use of maize for the production of artificial sweeteners, has also boosted demand for this product category. However, demand for animal feed in developing countries is becoming increasingly important, now accounting for over 40 per cent of global feed demand (increased from 37 per cent over ten years and from 25 per cent 20 years ago). This is projected to rise to 56 per cent by 2050. Use of coarse grains for biofuels has also expanded at a very rapid rate. However, given the peculiarly artificial nature of this demand, and extremely rapid developments in technology and policy in this area, the continuing impact of these changes on demand is very difficult to establish.

These broad patterns of dietary adjustment also include a definite move towards higher consumption of livestock products, meat and dairy products (Popkin, 1993; Popkin et al., 2012; Azuike et al., 2011). However, there is also wide diversity across countries here. In the case of meat, many countries have had traditionally very high levels of consumption, such as the traditional beef exporters (for example, Argentina, Uruguay) or those with a predominantly pastoral economy (for example, Mongolia). Recent developments, however, have been dominated by changes in the larger developing economies such as China, the Republic of Korea, Malaysia, Chile, Brazil and Saudi Arabia. In fact, the changes in China and Brazil have dominated the rise in per capita meat consumption in developing countries, which has risen from 14 kg per person per annum to 28 kg per person per annum between 1979–81 and 2005–07 (Alexandratos and Bruinsma, 2012). If consumption in these countries is excluded from the calculations, estimated average per capita consumption in this group of countries has shown a more modest increase from 12 kg to just over 17 kg per person per annum.

As of 2005–07, there were only 15 out of 98 developing countries consuming more than 50 kg meat per capita each year; this includes China and Brazil, which between them account for over 56 per cent of total meat consumption in this group of countries, though they account for only around 28 per cent of population. As many as 36 developing countries are projected to reach this level of consumption by 2050, increasing the weight of this group of countries in the calculation of global average consumption. As more countries begin to consume at medium to high per capita levels, and consumption increases to levels approaching those in the developed countries, it is likely that growth in global demand for meat will slow down as consumption reaches satiation levels in those countries.

Consumption of vegetable oils and other oil-crop products has also increased rapidly in developing countries. This has been a significant factor in the increase in average energy consumption per person per day for these countries, from around 5 kg per person per year in the 1970s to around 10 kg per person per year currently. At the same time, the contribution of these products to food consumption in developing countries is projected to increase from around 10 per cent of diets in 2005–07 to around 13 per cent by 2050.

Roots, tubers and plantains have been a major source of energy in diets of people living in Sub-Saharan Africa and Latin America. This includes 16 countries in Sub-Saharan Africa, where these products account for 20 per cent or more of calories consumed, rising to around 50 per cent for a small number of these countries. However, with the exception of potatoes, global consumption per capita of products in this group has tended to decline over time, principally driven by significant reductions in the consumption of sweet potatoes in China. These reductions may be bottoming out, and there have been significant increases in the productivity of other roots and tubers such as yams and cassava. Therefore, consumption and demand for these crops may begin to increase as other countries in Africa begin to replicate the experience of countries like Nigeria, Malawi and Ghana that have increased average food consumption and calorie intake by rapidly increasing production and consumption of these crops. Increased demand in East and South-East Asian countries is also possible as these crops, particularly cassava and sweet potatoes, are used to meet a rapidly rising demand for industrial starch and animal feed (Fuglie, 2004).

In the case of sugar, global average consumption per capita has been more or less constant over recent decades, the outcome of a balancing process between falling per capita consumption in developed countries and rising consumption in developing countries. In these countries, sugar has become an important source of calories, similar to the case of vegetable oils. Sugar is also a major export for some of these countries dominated by Brazil, but also including Thailand, Guatemala and Colombia. A number of other countries have become net importers in recent decades, for example, Nigeria, Indonesia, the Republic of Korea and Pakistan, so the scope for growth in consumption remains significant.

Biofuels, overall food requirements and the demand for food

The discussion and analysis in the previous section suggest that the capacity of the global agricultural system has been sufficient to meet the increased demand for food, generated by the main drivers (population, affluence, urbanisation etc.) since at least the 1960s. Evidence of food scarcity, in particular, evidence based on increases in food prices, is manifestly not available. For example, food prices declined over many decades up to the mid-1980s and then remained virtually constant until about 2005. The recent upsurge and instability have been attributed, among other factors, to the expansion in food demand arising from the increased use of feedstock for biofuels, particularly corn and oilseed (HLPE, 2013). This constitutes evidence that the food system has been demand constrained during most of this time, notwithstanding the abundant and equally compelling evidence that around one billion people were suffering from chronic food shortage throughout this period.

As discussed in previous sections of this chapter, food-related demand is projected to continue increasing up to 2050 at a decreasing rate. This assumes that population growth rates are declining and that population will reach a peak and begin to decline in some countries (such as Japan, Europe, China, Brazil) within this time span. It is also assumed that some countries will reach satiation levels for per capita consumption of some food products (such as meat) beyond which further increases in demand are attenuated. This will be accompanied by dietary shifts away from roots and tubers and towards increased consumption of fruit, vegetables, meat and dairy products. However, growth in total demand for food crops may not decline if the non-food demand for these commodities, for example, as feedstock for biofuels, continues to expand.

Biofuels now account for a significant proportion of the demand for maize (ethanol production in US), sugar cane (ethanol production in Brazil) and oilseed (biodiesel production in EU). Recent estimates suggest 127 million tonnes of maize is now used for this purpose, amounting to over 15 per cent of global maize production. Similarly, the use of sugar cane in Brazil accounts for nearly 16 per cent of global sugar cane production, and significant amounts of vegetable oils are being converted to biodiesel.

The key issues here relate to the creation and support of markets for biofuel products. These products compete directly with food products through their demand for feedstocks (maize, sugar cane and sugar beet for ethanol production; oilseeds for the production of biodiesel). They also compete through their demand for resources, principally land and water. Markets for these products are created and supported by a variety of government interventions employing a variety of policy tools (Su et al., 2015). These include tax exemptions for the blending of biofuels with fossil fuels, directly mandated blending requirements, public procurement of biofuels and vehicles and the provision of incentives to users such as subsidies for car fleet operators. At the same time, the supply of biofuels is directly encouraged by support for production and distribution that includes blending subsidies, subsidies for biofuel crops, subsidies for investment in biofuel production and distribution chain infrastructure and public support for research and development. There are also measures that regulate trade by limiting imports or exports using tariffs, quotas and other measures.

The significant increases in food prices in 2007/08 were substantively attributable to these policies even if other factors were also influential (HLPE, 2011). Many policy makers regard this coupling of the energy market and the food market as undesirable, not least because it means that variations in energy prices, possibly arising from speculative activity in energy markets, may now influence food prices. As a result, a number of changes are now being actively implemented to promote decoupling of these markets to some significant extent. This involves both the promotion of technological changes that will encourage a switch to energy feedstocks that compete less directly with food crops and the resources needed for food production (UNCTAD, 2016), as well as policy changes that reduce the attractiveness of using conventional food-competitive feedstocks (HLPE, 2013).

Competition between demand for biofuel feedstocks and demand for food, and the consequent concerns for the food security impact of biofuel support policies, depends on a range of factors (Koizumi, 2015; HLPE, 2013; Fischer et al., 2009). These will include the specific feedstocks involved, the extent to which these compete with food and feed crops for resources (particularly land and water), the relative efficiencies of the feedstocks in terms of yields, costs and greenhouse gas emissions and the particular processing technologies adopted. This competition has raised significant concerns in the case of conventional first generation biofuel technologies that rely on maize, sugar crops and oilseeds, since these compete directly with food and feed products. Ongoing technological developments are providing pathways for the conversion of alternative feedstocks, including those based on cellulosic material that, at least in principle, would not compete with food production. However, progress on this front has mainly been disappointing (Sims et al., 2010), though some recent developments in second-generation cellulosic alcohol production are becoming commercially available (UNCTAD, 2016, Nguyen et al., 2017).

Given the uncertainty about the continuing demand for biofuels as energy markets evolve, and about the extent to which this demand may lead to competition for food products, one popular scenario suggests that the impact expand until around 2020 and remain constant beyond that point.

On balance, these estimates suggest that by 2050 annual consumption of around 3.0 billion tonnes of cereals and 455 million tonnes of meat would be sufficient to provide more than adequate nourishment for the anticipated population level.[1] This would involve 1.8 billion tonnes of cereals and 317 million tonnes of meat produced in developing countries, with the remaining 40 per cent of cereals and 30 per cent of meat produced in developed countries (Alexandratos and Bruinsma, Table 4.1). This entails a 60 per cent increase in total agricultural output from 2005/07 levels, comprising a 77 per cent increase in developing countries and a 24 per cent increase in developed countries.

Resources, productivity and yields

Our ability to feed an expanding global population has been a matter for debate extending over past centuries. As pointed out by Alexandratos and Bruinsma (2012), there is early evidence on this debate in the writings of Tertullian in the 3rd century AD, with Malthus (1798) and Ehrlich (1968) providing more modern interpretations of the same set of issues. The common conclusions from these analyses is that population growth is inevitable, and the structure of physical and economic processes, and the relationship between them, is such that the rate of population growth and the increasing demand for food must outstrip and overwhelm our ability to produce food. The fact that this conclusion has been demonstrated to be incorrect in the centuries and decades following the publication of each of these studies seems to be forever obscured by the rhetoric of impending disaster and the call for ever more severe interventions to control population levels, usually those in developing countries. We discussed these issues in some detail in a previous section of this chapter.

In fact, world food production has grown faster than population throughout this period, allowing an overall increase in consumption per capita, while the rate of population growth has been slowing down. Global population grew from 2.5 billion in 1950 to 3.7 billion in 1970, reaching 6.9 billion in 2010. With population projected to expand to around 9.7 billion by 2050, this 2.8 billion increase over the 40-year period 2010 to 2050 is clearly lower than the increase of 3.2 billion from 1970 to 2010. This decelerating population growth is a key factor in the projected increases in food requirements above and provides a margin of flexibility for the production estimates discussed in this section.

However, global population and incomes are still increasing so an important set of issues here relate to tighter resource constraints and slower growth in yields and productivity, giving rise to concerns about having sufficient growth in food production to provide food security for our growing more affluent population. With this in mind, we consider the potential availability, for food production over coming decades, of land, water, fertiliser and crop protection chemicals.

Land, water and irrigation

With the benefit of modern satellite technology, we can say with some confidence that the land surface of the world extends to some 13.3 billion hectares. We are also confident that about 4.5 billion hectares of land are suitable for food production (Fischer et al., 2002, 2012), and no more than 1.3 billion hectares of this land (29 per cent) is currently in use for rain-fed and irrigated crops, leaving a balance of approximately 3.2 billion hectares. There are, however, a number of reasons why we cannot consider all of this land as being potentially available for crop production: for example, 1.8 billion hectares of this land is currently occupied, either by non-agricultural activities such as settlements, transport and communication infrastructure etc. or by forests and other protected areas. This means that there are approximately 1.4 billion hectares of "prime" land and "good" land on which additional crop production can be considered. This is land that has been judged very suitable, suitable, or moderately suitable for the rain-fed production of cereals, roots and tubers, sugar crops, pulses[2] and oil-bearing crops (Fischer et al., 2012). The distribution of this land across country groups and regions (Table 3.2) shows that there are approximately 960 million hectares (nearly 69 per cent) of this land available in developing countries and the remaining 440 million hectares (31 per cent) are in developed countries.

However, there are a number of critical constraints that must be taken into account when we consider the extent to which this land can contribute to relieving food insecurity across the world. Firstly, this land "reserve" is very unevenly distributed across countries and regions. For example, of the 960 million hectares in developing countries, approximately 85 per cent is located in Sub-Saharan Africa (450 million hectares) and Latin America (360 million hectares). This effectively means that there is no prime land or good land available for additional production

Table 3.2 Summary of land available by country group

Region	Total Land	Suitable Land[1]	Used for Crops (1999/2001)			Non-Agricultural Use[2]	Available for Crops and Pasture	%
			Rain-fed	Irrigated	Total			
WORLD	13295	4495	1063	197	1260	1824	1411	31
Developing Countries	7487	2893	565	138	703	1227	963	33
Sub-Saharan Africa	2281	1073	180	3	183	438	452	42
Latin America	2022	1095	137	15	152	580	363	33
Near East/North Africa	1159	95	38	12	50	9	36	38
South Asia	411	195	85	55	140	43	12	6
East Asia	1544	410	122	53	175	140	95	23
Other Developing Countries	70	25	2	0	2	16	7	28
Developed Countries	5486	1592	497	58	555	590	447	28
Other Countries	322	11	2	0	2	7	2	18

Source: Based on Fischer et al. (2012), Alexandratos and Bruinsma (2012), FAOSTAT (2015)

1 Includes land considered suitable for growing cereals, roots, tubers, sugar crops, pulses and oil-bearing crops.
2 Includes land under forest, under urban or industrial buildings and land under strict protection.

in many countries across the Near East and North Africa, South Asia and in Central America and the Caribbean. Furthermore, even in relatively land-abundant regions, there is significant variation in availability of reserve land across individual countries and sub-regions.

In addition, data on land suitability are based on the notion of "suitability" for the production of specific crops: cereals, roots and tubers, sugar crops, pulses, oil bearing crops. Land is counted as suitable when any one of these crops can be grown, irrespective of the extent to which this crop might or might not contribute to relieving food insecurity in the current circumstances. For example, the data indicates the suitability of large tracts of land in North Africa for growing only olives. Given the current abundance of olives in this area and the total unsuitability of much of this land for the cultivation of any other food crops, one may question whether this land, even if considered suitable under the accepted criteria, can, in reality, contribute to food production for the relief of hunger.

A further consideration is that there are usually good reasons why much of this land is currently not used for agricultural production. These can include constraints such as ecological fragility, low fertility, high levels of degradation and/or toxicity, high incidence of disease or lack of suitable infrastructure for access to input markets and output markets. The need to relieve these constraints by the use of high input levels and advanced management skills, and the need for high levels of investment to improve accessibility or to counteract diseases, can make using this land uneconomic under the prevailing incentive structures. For example, Fischer et al. (2002) note that around 70 per cent of the land potentially available for rain-fed agricultural production in Sub-Saharan Africa and the Caribbean is known to be subject to at least one constraint arising from soil or terrain characteristics. These problems, and the cost of overcoming them, should be considered when determining the availability of additional land for expanding agricultural production activities and output.

Therefore, it should not be concluded that availability of cropland does not pose a constraint on producing the additional food needed to meet the projected increases in food requirements. As already noted above, the need for investment in infrastructure is often a major constraint here, and there may be other constraints, such as incidence of disease, that need to be overcome before agricultural production is economically viable on this land. An additional factor that needs to be considered is that this reserve land is located in only a small number of countries (13 countries account for over 60 per cent of this land), and these are not necessarily the countries that are experiencing food shortages. So even with this relative abundance of arable land on a global basis, land constraints can be significantly binding at local or regional level, making discussion of the global availability of land less relevant to the immediate relief of food insecurity and hunger. However, the existence of this land will potentially lead to increased trade and might provide an incentive for overseas investment by those countries for which food production constraints are immediately binding – as evidenced by the recent increase of foreign investment in land in some developing countries, particularly in Africa (von Braun and Meinzen-Dick, 2009; Liversage, 2011). Ultimately, the existence of potentially exploitable land in a location at some distance from that of greatest need may lead to migration flows.

In these circumstances, it is not clear how much of this land might be used for agricultural production to meet the projected increases in food needs. The additional food will likely be provided by a combination of changes that could include increased yields, increased production intensity as well as expanding the area under cultivation. Estimates in the FAO study envisage a net additional 70 million hectares being used for crop production by 2050, a combination of reductions in developed countries (of around 40 million hectares) and offsetting increases in developing countries, amounting to around 110 million hectares (Table 4.8, Alexandratos and Bruinsma). However, it is projected that harvested area will have increased by significantly more than this, as the practice of multiple cropping is adopted more widely in tropical and semi-tropical countries. Assuming this net expansion takes place only on prime and good lands, it will account for only a very small proportion of available cropland leaving just over1.3 billion hectares free for further expansion or other uses.

Irrigated production has made a significant contribution to global food security through the Green Revolution of the past decades, in combination with the major increases in crop yields based on agricultural research and development. An important point is that, because yields on irrigated land are already very much greater than yields on rain-fed land, an increase in the availability of irrigated land, even without any further increases in yields, would lead to a significant increase in food production and a measurable increase in average yields.

There are approximately 300 million hectares equipped for irrigation and around 70 per cent of this land is in Asia (FAO, 2011). However, the potential for expanding irrigation is quite limited, principally because of the way in which water resources are distributed around the world. The availability of sufficient quantities of renewable water resources on a global basis is not in question. However, these resources are extremely limited in those areas where they are most needed (for example in the Near East, North Africa and Northern China), areas where there are significant amounts of potentially fertile land on which productivity is currently limited by availability of water during the growing season. In addition, any attempt to estimate availability of renewable water resources must also consider the extreme uncertainty surrounding estimates of potential uses of this water other than food production, for example, use for industrial purposes or to support urban residential uses, including uses related to recreation and tourism. The potential impacts of climate change must also be factored into these estimates, introducing a further element of uncertainty.

Alexandratos and Bruinsma (2012) estimate that there are approximately 180 million additional hectares in developing countries that could support expansion in irrigated production beyond the 235 million hectares already equipped for irrigation in these countries. They estimate that no more than 20 million hectares of this potential reserve will be pressed into service by 2050, leading to a net expansion to 255 million hectares in these countries, 320 million hectares globally. However, to maintain this area of land equipped and usable for irrigation will require gross investment in irrigation facilities at a level much higher than that implied by this relatively modest net expansion in irrigated area, since much of the existing irrigation equipment will need to be refurbished or replaced due to degradation and increasing water shortages.

Most currently irrigated land is in developing countries, where it accounts for around 40 per cent of area under cereals and nearly 60 per cent of cereals output. Nearly half of this land is in India and China, and it is projected that around one third of the expected expansion in irrigated area will be in these two countries. Pressure on water resources is not apparent at global level, but availability of sufficient renewable water resources to support the proposed expansion in irrigated area is extremely limited in some regions. While water withdrawal for irrigation is less than 7 per cent of globally available renewable water (HLPE, 2015), it amounts to over 50 per cent of that available in the Near East and North Africa and around 40 per cent of availability in South Asia. Moreover, these percentages are being exceeded in some individual countries, even in regions where overall use is well below these levels (for example, in some Central American countries). Given natural variability in water availability, it is generally agreed that any country using more than 20 per cent of its renewable water resources for irrigation could be moving towards water scarcity. Currently, 22 countries have crossed this threshold, and 13 of these have exceeded the more critical 40 per cent usage level. It is also estimated that four countries in the Middle East and North Africa (Saudi Arabia, Yemen, Egypt and Libya) are using more than 100 per cent of their renewable water for irrigation, in effect 'mining' their ground water reserves. Exploiting whatever potential exists for improving efficiency of irrigation water use is critical for these and a number of other countries to continue maintaining their current irrigated area, but this will not likely provide any flexibility for expanding this area.

Availability of fertiliser and crop protection chemicals

The availability of fertilisers, chemicals and irrigation facilities has been one of the keys to the success of the original Green Revolution that has transformed food security over recent decades. This has mainly been effective through impact on yields, allowing significant increases in production without major expansion in land used.

Estimates suggest that 40 per cent of the increase in per capita food production that was achieved in the latter half of the 20th century can be largely attributed to increased use of nitrogen fertiliser (Smil, 2002). Half of the increase in grain production in India and one-third of global increases in grain production during the 1970s and 1980s have been similarly attributed to increases in total fertiliser use, potassium (K) and phosphate (P), as well as nitrogen (N). As production increases in the decades towards 2050 further increases in fertiliser use is expected.

According to Alexandratos and Bruinsma (2012), global fertiliser use is projected to increase by nearly 60 per cent to 263 million tonnes by 2050 (from 166 million tonnes in 2005/07), and this would actually entail a slowing down in annual growth in fertiliser use. This slow-down in fertiliser use, illustrated in

Table 3.3, is attributable to a number of factors, including the gradual slow-down in growth in crop production discussed in earlier sections of this chapter. Reaction to the negative environmental impacts of intensive fertiliser use, the increasing popularity of organic agriculture and the use of non-mineral sources of nutrients are also important.

Nitrogen fertiliser is usually derived from industrial sources, relying on the availability of fossil fuels (principally natural gas) both as a raw material and as a source of energy for the transformation processes involved. Atmospheric nitrogen is also used as a raw material. Crop protection chemicals also rely on fossil fuels for raw materials and energy. According to the US Geological Survey (2016), the availability of these materials is considered sufficient to support current levels of global food production and expected production into the future. Potassium, on the other hand, is dependent on natural sources, principally deposits available for mining and salt-rich lakes where potassium can be refined from natural salt deposits. The separation and refinement of material suitable for use as fertiliser is an energy intensive industrial process. Current estimates suggest that there are adequate supplies of raw materials to support current annual production rates for more than 250 years. Phosphate is similarly reliant on natural deposits in the form of phosphate rock and also depends on an energy intensive industrial process to transform the mined material into material suitable for use as a fertiliser. The US Geological Survey (2016) expects current known reserves to support current and expected rates of production for around 300 years.

Yield and productivity trends

Increasing yields have been the principal factor that has underpinned the continual and substantial reductions in global food insecurity for at least five decades. For example, average cereal yields increased from 1.44 tonnes per hectare in the early 1960s, to 2.4 tonnes in 1980s, reaching 3.4 tonnes in 2005/07. However, as pointed out by Alexandratos and Bruinsma (2012) and by Alston and Pardey (2014), this trajectory corresponds to an approximately constant annual increment of around 44 kg/hectare each year, which implies a declining annual rate of growth; 44 kg per year amounts to 3.1 per cent of 1.44 tonnes, 1.8 per cent of 2.4

Table 3.3 Growth in fertiliser use 1961/63 to 2005/07 and projections to 2050

Region	Million Tonnes Nutrient (N, P and K)			Per cent per annum		
	1961/63	*2005/07*	*2050*	*1997–2007*	*2005/07–2030*	*2030–2050*
World	34.3	166.0	263.0	2.4	1.4	0.7
Developing Countries	4.3	114.0	201.0	3.8	1.7	0.8
Developed Countries	30.0	51.0	62.0	−0.3	0.6	0.3

Source: Based on Table 4.15 in Alexandratos and Bruinsma (2012)

tonnes, reducing to around 1.3 per cent of 3.4 tonnes. Nevertheless, this continued annual increase in yield, even if declining from year to year, is sufficient to meet projected demands for 2050. Average yields would have increased to around 5.42 tonnes per hectare by that time, and world production at 3.8 billion tonnes would exceed the projected demand of 3.28 billion tonnes.

However, this does not mean that investments to increase yields, or to improve agricultural and rural infrastructure, are less urgent or no longer necessary. Given the uncertainty surrounding these estimates, any improvement in agricultural productivity growth would make it easier to achieve the levels of production needed to meet projected food requirements.

For example, genetic engineering has begun to contribute to the stability of yields, in some environments, by providing herbicide tolerance and resistance to some insect damage. In addition, tolerance to drought, high temperatures, salinity and other hazards, as well as direct enhancement of yields through nitrogen fixation and more efficient photosynthesis, are longer-term prospects (Godfray et al., 2010). Furthermore, a meta-analysis by Klumper and Qaim (2014) of recent studies of the impacts of genetically modified crops has provided robust evidence that adoption of herbicide tolerant and/or insect-resistant varieties of maize, soybeans and cotton has benefited farmers in developed as well as developing countries. These benefits have included 37 per cent reduction in pesticide use, 22 per cent increase in crop yields and increased farmer profits of 68 per cent. A significant proportion of these gains are being achieved as spin-offs from commercially funded research, where commercial gains are the principal motivation. In these circumstances, an increase in public funding would encourage research that generates broader public benefits and enhances welfare gains for farmers and consumers.

At the same time, policies to close existing gaps between yields achieved by different producers with similar land and other resources (for example, through programmes to promote adoption of new crop varieties and modern farming practices) have often been proposed as a straightforward approach to increasing output. However, potential contributions are often limited by what is economically feasible from a whole-farm management point of view, especially when the producers are already seeking to balance the productivity, profitability and riskiness in their existing farming operations (Sadras et al., 2015).

The slow-down in the growth of productivity in agricultural production has also been investigated at global level and, for some individual countries and regions, using an alternative measure, 'total factor productivity' (TFP). This is based on comparing change in the use of all inputs and the resulting change in production of all outputs over a period. This is a broader measure of productivity than change in yield, where we compare change in land use and change in the output of a single crop or a limited number of related crops. The outcomes of these TFP studies have been mixed. For example, Fuglie (2012) concludes that there has not been a slow-down in the growth rate of global agricultural productivity; productivity growth may even have accelerated in recent decades, driven by advances in Brazil and China. However, these results remain controversial (Alston and Pardey, 2014).

Trends in production

As noted in the previous section, we expect the overall demand for food to continue increasing at slower rates than in the past, mainly driven by the slowing down in population growth and higher proportions of the world's population reaching satiation levels of food consumption, i.e. levels closer to those in many developed countries. On this basis, a continuing but decelerating growth in the demand for food is expected to persist to mid-century.

However, we have not fully factored in the impact of the emerging market for bioenergy, mainly because of the significant uncertainties surrounding the continuing demand for food and feed crops as feedstock for bioenergy production. This means that the projections in food demand assume that the energy-driven demand for these crops continues to increase until 2020 and remains static after that time. This is, of course, a compromise solution, and it may not reflect the actual trajectory of demand as technologies, policies and the energy market itself changes over the next decades.

With this in mind, demand for crop and livestock products is expected to grow at a rate of 1.1 per cent per annum for the 2005/07–2050 period, down from around 2 per cent per annum over recent decades. While the reduction in the growth rate of population is partly responsible for this slow-down, the reduction in the growth of consumption per capita in developing countries is also a significant factor. This is principally, but not entirely, driven by the reduced growth rate in food demand experienced in China and Brazil as consumption levels begin to approach levels typically found in more developed countries.

Crop production

The projections used here are based on those provided by FAO (Alexandratos and Bruinsma, 2012) for 34 crops across 105 countries and country groups, with separate projections for production on rain-fed land and on irrigated land. Data on area, yields and production of each crop in each country are assembled from a variety of published and unpublished sources and supplemented by expert judgement to ensure consistency and coherence between estimates of total arable area, total harvested area of crops, total production and estimated yields from these different sources. Starting with these baseline estimates, projected crop production for 2030 and 2050 are converted into combinations of harvested area and yield for rain-fed and irrigated land, consistent with estimates for total arable area and irrigated area. This information is provided for most crops in the Global Agro-Ecological Zone (GAEZ) study (Fischer et al., 2002) and is regularly updated (Fischer et al., 2012). This data is used in deriving the estimates discussed here.

The general pattern, of continued but decelerating growth, reflecting both the pattern of population growth highlighted earlier in this chapter and the pattern of growth in total agricultural output above, is illustrated in Table 3.4. This slow-down, apparent across all regions of the world, is particularly pronounced for developed countries where growth rates of less than 0.5 per cent per annum are

Table 3.4   Annual crop production growth (per cent per annum)

Area/Region	1961–2007	1987–2007	1997–2007	2007–2030	2030–2050
World	2.2	2.3	2.3	1.3	0.7
Developing Countries	3.0	3.1	3.0	1.4	0.8
(Developing Countries excluding India and China)	2.8	2.8	3.2	1.7	1.0
Sub-Saharan Africa	2.6	3.3	3.0	2.4	1.9
Latin America and the Caribbean	2.7	2.9	3.7	1.7	0.7
Near East/North Africa	2.9	2.5	2.4	1.4	0.9
South Asia	2.6	2.4	2.1	1.5	0.9
East Asia	3.4	3.6	3.2	1.1	0.3
Developed Countries	0.8	0.4	0.5	0.8	0.3
44 Countries with over 2770 kcal/ person in 2007 (and 57 per cent of world population)	2.6	2.9	2.1	1.1	0.4

Source: Based on Table 4.3 in Alexandratos and Bruinsma (2012)

projected for the two decades 2030 to 2050. Nevertheless, projected growth rates in crop output remain positive over this entire period.

Summary results of an analysis of sources of growth from this study are shown in Table 3.5, based on an analysis of the aggregate (price weighted) production and yields of the 34 individual crops analysed. The results show that nearly 80 per cent of the projected increase in crop output in developing countries is attributable to intensification, with 73 per cent due to yield increase and a further 6 per cent to increase in multi-cropping (cropping intensity). The share due to yield increase expands to around 90 per cent in a group of 19 land-scarce countries (currently using more than 60 per cent of their available arable land) and falls to 59 per cent in a group of 24 land-rich countries (currently using less than 40 per cent of their available arable land).

In developed countries the area of land in crop production has been declining since the mid-1980s, so growth in crop yields has been the main source of both increased output and the additional output required to compensate for the output from land lost to degradation, urbanisation etc. From a global perspective, this means that intensification (either by increase in yield or increased cropping intensity) is seen to account for over 90 per cent of the increase in output over the projection period. Yield increase is also the principal contributor to output expansion in wheat and rice, particularly in the land-scarce regions of Asia and Near East/North Africa, where significant amounts of these crops are grown. On the other hand, maize is mainly grown in the more land-abundant areas of Latin America and Sub-Saharan Africa, so expansion in land use has been a more important driver of output expansion for this crop, and this is expected to continue into the projection period.

The difference between maize (and other coarse grains) on the one hand, and wheat and rice on the other, is further accentuated by the differences in end use

Table 3.5   Sources of growth in crop production (per cent)

Area/Region	Arable Land Expansion		Increased Cropping Intensity		Yield Increases	
	1961– 2007	2007– 2050	1961– 2007	2007– 2050	1961– 2007	2007– 2050
All Developing Countries	23	21	8	6	70	73
Sub-Saharan Africa	31	20	31	6	38	74
Latin America and the Caribbean	40	40	7	7	53	53
Near East/North Africa	17	0	22	20	62	80
South Asia	6	6	12	2	82	92
East Asia	28	0	−6	15	77	85
Land-Rich Developing Countries		35		6		59
Land-Poor Developing Countries		4		6		90
World	14	10	9	10	77	80

Source: Based on Table 4.4 in Alexandratos and Bruinsma, 2012

and the growing importance of the nutrition transition. This means that an increasing proportion of the increase in the production of maize and other coarse grains will be used as livestock feed. As a result, maize production in developing countries is projected to increase by 1.4 per cent per annum with corresponding projections of 0.9 per cent for wheat and 0.6 per cent for rice. In China, these results are particularly stark; wheat and rice production are projected to grow marginally to 2030 and decline after that, whereas maize production continues to grow throughout the projection period. These patterns will be reflected in land allocation, with increasing shares of arable land allocated to the production of maize and other coarse grains.

The role of irrigated land and the contribution of irrigated production to the overall expansion in output are also relevant here. Current estimates suggest that irrigated agriculture, on about 16 per cent of available arable land, accounts for approximately 44 per cent of all crop production (42 per cent of cereal production) across all countries of the world. For developing countries, the data suggests that 21 per cent of the land is irrigated and this accounts for 49 per cent of all crop production (60 per cent of cereal production). These shares are not expected to change over the projection period.

Livestock production

Growth in livestock production over recent decades, and growth projected to 2050, follows similar patters to those observed for total agricultural output; production continues to increase as growth rates remain positive but continue to decline. This slowing down in growth is more marked in developed countries than in developing countries.

It is also the case that the decline in growth rates in livestock production is less than that observed for crop production. The share of livestock products in the diet continues to increase in many countries, especially developing countries, so the difference between livestock production and crop production is more marked in these countries. These patterns are illustrated in the data presented in Table 3.6.

As in the case of crop production, increased livestock production can be achieved through expansion in scale (in this case increase in livestock numbers) or by increasing productivity. Productivity can be increased through a combination of increasing "off-take rates" by shortening the production cycle (e.g., speeding up the animal fattening process), or by increasing carcass weight or annual yield of milk per animal or eggs per bird. For the FAO projections being discussed here, there is a significant contribution from increased livestock numbers, with carcass weight also playing a role in expanding beef and mutton production, and shorter production cycles becoming more important in poultry and pig meat production. These differences are highlighted in the data presented in Table 3.7

The impact of climate change

The impact of climate change has not been factored into the analysis in this study, mainly because of time limitations and the need for a much more comprehensive treatment than would have been possible with the resources available. Only a brief summary of a few key studies is presented here. One emerging theme from these studies is that there are major impacts on crop yields, and these are likely to be related to a wide range of changes including increased temperatures, increased concentrations of atmospheric CO_2 and increased frequency and intensity of

Table 3.6 Annual livestock production growth (per cent per annum)

Area/Region	1961– 2007	1987– 2007	1997– 2007	2007– 2030	2030– 2050
World	2.2	2.0	2.0	1.4	0.9
Developing Countries	4.3	4.5	3.4	2.0	1.3
(Developing Countries excluding India and China)	3.4	3.6	3.5	2.1	1.5
Sub-Saharan Africa	2.5	2.8	3.3	2.7	2.6
Latin America and the Caribbean	3.2	3.8	3.8	1.6	0.9
Near East/North Africa	3.3	3.3	3.0	2.2	1.7
South Asia	3.7	3.6	3.2	2.7	2.2
East Asia	6.5	5.9	3.4	1.8	0.8
Developed Countries	1.0	−0.1	0.6	0.6	0.2
44 Countries with over 2770 kcal/ person in 2007 (and 57 per cent of world population)	2.7	2.9	1.8	1.1	0.5

Source: Based on Table 4.17 in Alexandratos and Bruinsma, 2012;

1 Aggregate livestock production is calculated by weighting the four meat products (beef, mutton, pig meat and poultry meat), milk products and eggs using 2004/06 international commodity prices.

Table 3.7 World livestock production by livestock sector

Sector	1961/63	2005/07	2050	1961–2007	1987–2007	1997–2007	2005/07–2050
	Million tonnes			Annual Growth Rate (% per annum)			
Total Meat	72	258	455	2.9	2.5	2.2	1.3
Beef	30	64	106	1.6	0.9	1.2	1.2
Mutton	6	13	25	1.7	1.8	2.1	1.5
Pig meat	26	100	143	3.1	2.3	1.7	0.8
Poultry meat	9	82	181	5.2	4.7	3.9	1.8
Milk	344	664	1077	1.4	1.3	2.2	1.1
Eggs	14	62	102	3.5	3.3	2.3	1.1

Source: Based on Table 4.18 in Alexandratos and Bruinsma, 2012;

weather events. For example, the FAO Interdepartmental Working Group on Climate Change (2008) looks at the impacts on food security that could arise through a wide variety of changes to the earth's atmosphere and its climate. These include impacts arising from increases in global mean temperatures, yield impacts of CO_2 fertilisation and effects on production of gradual changes in precipitation patterns. Changes in precipitation patterns lead to both increased frequency and increased intensity of droughts and to changes in the timing, location and amount of rain and snow. They also investigate how the availability of crop and livestock products is influenced by changes in frequency and intensity of extreme weather events, especially storms and floods, and by increases in weather variability. These changes are also the focus of HLPE (2012).

In fact, the Fifth Assessment Report of the Intergovernmental Panel on Climate Change (IPCC) emphasise the negative impact on the yields of major crops (wheat, maize, rice) of higher temperatures of around 30°C. The production of these crops is predicted to decline from around 2050 (Porter et al., 2014). IPCC also recognise the potentially positive impacts on the yields of these crops, of increased concentrations of atmospheric CO_2, and the potentially negative effects of increased ozone concentrations. In addition, they emphasise that impacts of these changes on nutritional quality, competition from weeds and disease intensity, though poorly understood, must also be considered. These effects are likely to have particular impact on Sub-Saharan Africa and the rice growing areas of South Asia, while food production and food quality are also at risk in Central and South America. However, it is likely that yields may increase in higher latitudes and that adaptation to climate change will be more effective in these areas.

IPCC (2015) point out that climate change will impact on all components of food security, not just on food production. Access and affordability (see Chapter 4) is becoming more important for a number of reasons. Firstly, for those who live in vulnerable areas the local effects of climate change will almost certainly increase their vulnerability. For example, changes in frequency and intensity of droughts are likely to have a particular impact on those whose livelihoods are based on livestock production in agro-pastoral areas, where existing transient poverty is likely to be transformed into chronic poverty. Secondly, impacts on stability of food production and potential impacts on the stability of food prices will also affect the livelihoods and access to food of those who are net food buyers, those who have migrated to urban areas, and those without access to production resources who continue to live in rural areas. Thirdly, impacts on food utilisation (see Chapter 5) are also possible through the effect of climate changes on the nutritional quality of the food produced, mainly through the impact of harsher climatic conditions on nutrient density and protein content of grains and other crops.

In reviewing these studies, it becomes clear that there is a very high level of uncertainty surrounding many of these estimates and this is explicitly recognised by IPCC by specifying a level of confidence associated with each estimate. They present the main estimates summarised here with Medium Confidence. They go on to explain, "confidence is an evaluation of the level of evidence and the degree of agreement of findings within the evidence. Medium confidence, therefore, may mean there is limited evidence with high agreement, or medium evidence with medium agreement, or robust evidence with limited agreement" (Mastrandrea et al., 2011). In fact, for changes up to around 2050, it is quite likely that the negative effects on crop yields and livestock output may be offset in large part by the impact of CO_2 fertilisation and the positive impact on yields in higher latitudes. The negative impact on yields and production is likely to be observable only after 2050. In part, this is a justification for not factoring the impact of climate change into our estimates of production levels up to 2050. However, concern remains for what happens after 2050.

There is also evidence that agricultural production represents one area of human activity that has both positive and negative influences on the rate of climate change through its effects on the level of greenhouse gases. Although the increase in the level of plant material associated with increasing intensity of agricultural production increases the amount of carbon sequestration, thus reducing atmospheric CO_2 concentrations, an important effect of agricultural production is acknowledged to be an increase in the concentration of greenhouse gases. This arises from a number of the processes associated with food production in a modern agricultural system. First, land use change arising from the expansion of agricultural production on land not previously cultivated results in the release of CO_2 into the atmosphere; this is a particular problem in the case of deforestation. Second, while nitrous oxides may be released spontaneously by soils, the intensification of agricultural production leads to a significant increase in these releases through mechanical cultivation, through use of animal manure as fertiliser and through using nitrogenous fertilisers. More importantly, there is also a major impact on greenhouse gases through the release of methane associated with livestock production and the production of rice in paddy fields. This is currently receiving a significant amount of attention following the recent discovery that atmospheric concentrations of methane have been increasing faster in the last few years than at any time in the past two decades. While the precise sources of these increases has not been determined, it is confidently expected that agriculture and, to a lesser extent, fossil fuel use and possibly wetlands, will prove to be the main sources (Saunois et al., 2016). The implication here is that the increasing intensity and extent of agricultural production, needed to maintain food security into the future, must be managed carefully to ensure that the impact on climate change and on the environment is minimised.

Trade and food availability

There is wide agreement among economists that open markets allowing unhindered trade flows among countries can be an important factor in raising production and incomes for food producers and in allocating production and productive resources to areas where they can be used most efficiently and most effectively (Brooks and Matthews, 2015; McCorriston et al., 2013). This will facilitate the flow of food products from surplus to deficit areas, contributing to net increases in food security and a decline in the prevalence of undernourishment.

Trade in food products is an important component of food availability at national level, influencing the distribution of food between countries. In addition, trade influences the distribution of food supplies within countries, between urban and rural markets and between different points in time. This allows balancing available supplies between surplus and deficit countries and areas and between surplus and deficit seasons and years. In this way, trade can also affect the distribution of food within countries, both geographically and temporally. In responding to market price signals, trade can also stabilise food supplies by increasing availability in areas and at times/seasons when local supplies fall short.

A number of studies, including the FAO study discussed in earlier sections of this chapter (Alexandratos and Bruinsma, 2012), have indicated the increasing importance of trade as a support for food security. Moreover, they suggest that role of trade in distributing available food supplies will become more important rather than less important over time.

While trade can lead to improvements in food security, there are also circumstances in which deterioration is possible. When an increase in imports leads to improvements in food availability, this also increases reliance on external supplies and raises concerns about risk of these supplies being cut off. A key question is whether increased imports will displace domestic production, where imported food products compete with domestic production, reducing the profitability and numbers of domestic producers, or whether imports complement domestic production by responding to increases in demand and providing additional supplies that are not available from domestic producers. Reliance on external supplies is exacerbated in the former case.

One other issue related to food availability arises from the possibility that increased opportunities for trade will lead to a change in the pattern of production that leads to increased emphasis on exportable cash crops. If this is at the expense of food crops for the domestic markets, there are likely negative consequences for food security. However, where smallholders are part of a well-organised and well-integrated supply chain, producer incomes are likely increased to enable the purchase of increased amounts of a wider variety of food products (FAO, 2015; Negash and Swinnen, 2013; Wiggins et al., 2015). The proceeds from increased exports also contribute to balancing the cost of any required imports at national level, though these impacts vary widely across countries, emphasising the importance of considering the heterogeneity between countries in this discussion.

More importantly, it is emphasised by all studies that any expansion in trade of agricultural products will affect all four dimensions of food security, including food availability. Trade will influence the purchasing power of consumers and thus their ability to access food (see Chapter 4). In addition, trade will affect the variety of food products available to consumers and, depending on any specific changes in regulations as openness to trade increases, may increase or decrease food quality. These potential impacts on food utilisation are discussed in Chapter 5. Finally, the impact of trade on stability is based on its impact on volatility of food supplies, food prices, incomes, and food quality, and is closely related to impacts on the volatility of agricultural markets. We discuss these issues in Chapter 6.

Summary and implications for policy intervention

This chapter investigates how food requirements and food availability have grown over recent decades and how they are likely to evolve over the decades to 2050. The discussion focuses in particular on the balance between these processes, considering likely global food needs by 2050 and how this food can be produced given available resources and how these change over the period.

Population change is seen as a key driver and the population projections examined here highlight the continuing increase in population levels even as growth rates are reduced. The analysis focuses in particular on the continuing high rates of population increase that are concentrated in countries with limited resources to support necessary production or import of food. This emphasises the increased urgency for finding ways of feeding these hungry people.

The discussion highlights the evolving evidence that continues to undermine the popular Malthusian notions of starvation induced by population growth. The notions of Boserup and Simon emphasise the benefits of people as a resource that facilitates technical change, and points to a more positive role for people in the longer run. The message here is that people are not just mouths to feed – they are also brains that can think, minds that can create, as well as hands that can work

The chapter also pinpoints the effects of increased income arising from economic growth across the majority of countries, emphasising its dual role in alleviating poverty and improving food affordability (Chapter 4) on the one hand, and its contribution as one of the principal drivers of the nutrition transition on the other. Another driver of this process of dietary change, urbanisation, is also discussed.

The progress of the nutrition transition is considered in some detail, drawing attention to the reduction in consumption of roots and tubers (and to some extent cereals) and the increase in consumption of meat, milk products, eggs, and vegetable oils. The variable progress of this transition across different continents, and the impact of recent transitions in China and Brazil on average consumption levels, is particularly emphasised. Expected changes in food demand and the overall impact on food requirements are summarised.

The principal estimates suggest that annual production of around 3 billion tonnes of cereals and 455 million tonnes of meat will be needed to meet global food demand by 2050, representing an increase in overall production of around 60 per cent.

This chapter also explores in some detail the availability of sufficient land, water, fertiliser and other resources to support these increases in production. In recent decades, these resources, and the underpinning research and development, have allowed production to expand faster than the population has grown, enabling a significant increase in food availability per person. There would appear to be a substantial reserve of land suitable for food production that is not currently used for this purpose. This land is distributed unevenly across regions and continents, located in a small number of countries, most of which do not have food security problems. In addition, much of this land is already used for other purposes including forests that provide important carbon sequestration services and other globally important ecological services. Large tracts of the remaining land are subject to a range of problems arising from low fertility, degradation/toxicity, disease incidence or lack of suitable infrastructure for access. This means that this land can be made available for food production only after significant investment is made to alleviate these constraints. Economic incentives to support this investment may be lacking.

A similar pattern summarises the availability of fresh water – adequate availability at a global level, but very limited availability is areas where the need is greatest. Availability is particularly limited in areas such as the Near East, North Africa and Northern China, where there are significant amounts of potentially fertile land where productivity is limited mainly by water availability during the growing season.

Like water and irrigation, the use of chemical fertilisers and crop protection chemicals were central to the increased yields achieved during the Green Revolution of recent decades, so the continuing availability of these resources remains critical to achieving any future increase in yields and productivity. Current estimates suggest that availability of resources needed for these products, including reserves of phosphate and potassium raw materials, are adequate to support any foreseeable level of agricultural production over more than a century into the future.

Growth in agricultural productivity, while remaining positive, has been slowing down over recent decades. Nevertheless, this more slowly growing productivity has been judged to be adequate to support the levels of production needed to provide expected food requirements to 2050 without relying on new policy initiatives focused on 'closing the yield gap' or on research aimed at extending the potential of recent advances in genetic engineering. However, such changes would provide useful safety margins in this critical area.

Estimates of the potential impact of climate change are also considered here, mainly based on a recent FAO study and the more recent estimates from the IPCCs

Fifth Assessment Report. These studies emphasise that climate change is likely to affect all components of food security, not just food availability. Impacts on accessibility and affordability of food are also likely, through effects on livelihoods of vulnerable groups of people, as are impacts on food utilisation through effects on the nutritional quality of food, and impacts on stability of food production and prices. However, the studies also point out that impacts on food availability may be delayed for a number of decades. It is quite likely, for change up to around 2050, that the negative effects on yields and productivity of increased temperatures are likely to be offset by the positive effects of increased carbon dioxide concentrations.

This chapter also discusses the impact of increased openness to trade on food availability, emphasising the impact on incomes and productivity of food producers and the increased efficiency of resource use. The role of trade in balancing food availability and requirements both geographically and temporally are also emphasised. This includes transfers between deficit and surplus countries and sub-areas within countries as well as between deficit and surplus years and seasons. The potentially negative influences of increased openness to trade are also recognised, including potential displacement of domestic food production by cash crops and the dangers of increased reliance on external food supplies. The discussions summarised here also acknowledge that trade will affect all four dimensions of food security, not just food availability.

The estimates presented and discussed here suggest that the evolving trajectory of resources available for food production over the decades to 2050, are likely to be sufficient to meet projected food requirements. In other words, this analysis suggests that falling yield growth rates do not pose a problem for the ability of the current agricultural system to continue meeting the expanding aggregate demand for food. However, this does not mean that investment is not warranted in research and extension programmes to improve both potential yields and the yields achieved by producers. In particular, there is a need for public funding to complement the significant private commercial funding for research on genetically modified varieties of important food crops. Public and private investments are also needed for resource-poor countries with rapidly expanding demand for food in order to mitigate local constraints to growth in yields, to expand capacity for research and development and to improve transport and communication infrastructures as well as on-farm facilities.

However, having sufficient resources to produce these levels of output does not ensure that they will be produced. Actual production will depend on decisions by individual farmers and farm businesses about choosing appropriate production systems and managing productivity, profitability and risk and by applying the appropriate levels of inputs and investment. Motivating these decisions will require policies that promote the necessary incentives, as well as policies that sustain the financial and market infrastructure that facilitates efficient financing of investments and effective management of insurance and risk. It is particularly important that these policies be tailored to meet the needs of smallholders as well as those of large-scale commercial farmers.

Notes

1 Based on FAO estimates, this level of production would be capable of providing around 2,900 kilocalories per person per day for the projected 9.7 billion people in 2050. This compares to the current Minimum Dietary Energy Requirements of between 1,650 and 1,900 kilocalories per person per day, used by FAO in estimating the prevalence of undernutrition.
2 Pulse crops include peas, beans, chickpeas and lentils.

References

Alexandratos, N. and Bruinsma, J. 2012. *World Agriculture Towards 2030/2050: The 2012 Revision*. Rome: FAO.

Alston, J. M. and Pardey, P. G. 2014. Agriculture in the Global Economy. *Journal of Economic Perspectives*, 28, 121–146.

Azuike, E. C., Emelumadu, O. F., Adinma, E. D., Ifeadike, C. O., Ebenebe, U. E. and Adogu, P. U. 2011. Nutrition Transition in Developing Countries: A Review. *Afrimedic Journal*, 2, 1–5.

Beddington, J., Godfray, C., Crute, I., Haddad, L., Lawrence, D., Muir, J., Pretty, J., Robinson, S. and Toulmin, C. 2011. *Foresight. The Future of Food and Farming: Challenges and Choices for Global Sustainability*. London: Government Office for Science.

Boserup, E. 1965. *The Conditions for Agricultural Growth*. London: George Allen & Unwin.

Brandow, G. E. 1977. Policy for Commercial Agriculture. *In:* Martin, L. (ed.) *A Survey of Agricultural Economics Literature Volume 1*. Minneapolis: University of Minnesota Press.

Brooks, J. and Matthews, A. 2015. Trade Dimensions of Food Security. *OECD Food, Agriculture and Fisheries Papers, No 77*. Paris: OECD Publishing.

Connelly, M. 2008. *Fatal Misconceptions: The Struggle to Control World Population*. Boston: Harvard University Press.

Ehrlich, P. R. 1968. *The Population Bomb*. New York: Ballantine Books.

Ehrlich, P. R. and Ehrlich, A. H. 1992. The Value of Biodiversity. *Ambio*, 21, 219–226.

Erb, K., Haberl, H., Krausmann, F., Lauk, C., Plutzar, C., Steinberger, J., Muller, C., Bondeau, A., Waha, K. and Pollack, G. 2009. Eating the Planet: Feeding and Fuelling the World Sustainably, Fairly and Humanely – A Scoping Study. *Institute of Social Ecology, Klagenfurt University, Social Ecology Working Paper 116*.

FAO. 2011. *The State of the World's Land and Water Resources for Food and Agriculture (SOLAW) – Managing Systems at Risk*. Rome and London: FAO and Earthscan.

FAO. 2015. *The State of Agricultural Commodity Markets: Trade and Food Security: Achieving a Better Balance Between National Priorities and the Collective Good*. Rome: FAO.

FAO Interdepartmental Working Group on Climate Change. 2008. *Climate Change and Food Security: A Framework Document*. Rome: FAO.

Fischer, G., Hizsnyik, E., Prieler, S., Shah, M. and Van Velthuizen, H. T. 2009. Biofuels and Food Security. *Report to Sponsor: The OPEC Fund for International Development (OFID)*. Vienna: IIASA.

Fischer, G., Nachtergaele, F. O., Prieler, S., Teixeira, E., Toth, G., Van Velthuizen, H., Verelst, L. and Wiberg, D. 2012. *Global Agro-ecological Zones: Model Documentation GAEZ ver 3.0*. Rome/Laxenberg: FAO/IIASA.

Fischer, G., Van Velthuizen, H., Shah, M. and Nachtergaele, F. 2002. *Global Agro-Ecological Assessment for Agriculture in the 21st Century: Methodology and Results*. Rome and Laxenberg: FAO/IIASA.

Fuglie, K. O. 2004. Challenging Bennett's Law: The New Economics of Starchy Staples in Asia. *Food Policy*, 29, 187–202.

Fuglie, K. O. 2012. Productivity Growth and Technology Capital in the Global Agricultural Economy. *In:* Fuglie, K. O., Wang, S. L. and Ball, E. V. (eds.) *Productivity Growth in Agriculture: An International Perspective*. Oxfordshire, UK: CAB International.

Gardner, B. L. 1992. Changing Economic Perspectives on the Farm Problem. *Journal of Economic Literature*, XXX, 62–101.

Godfray, H. C. J., Beddington, J. R., Crute, I. R., Haddad, L., Lawrence, D., Muir, J. F., Pretty, J., Robinson, S., Thomas, S. M. and Toulmin, C. 2010. Food Security: The Challenge of Feeding 9 Billion People. *Science*, 327, 812–818.

Gollin, D., Lagakos, D. and Waugh, M. E. 2014. The Agricultural Productivity Gap. *Quarterly Journal of Economics*, 129, 939–993.

HLPE. 2011. Price Volatility and Food Security. *Report of the High Level Panel of Experts on Food Security and Nutrition of the Committee on World Food Security*. Rome.

HLPE. 2012. Food Security and Climate Change. *Report of the High Level Panel of Experts on Food Security and Nutrition of the Committee on World Food Security*. Rome.

HLPE. 2013. Biofuels and Food Security. *Report of the High Level Panel of Experts on Food Security and Nutrition of the Committee on World Food Security*. Rome.

HLPE. 2015. Water for Food Security and Nutrition. *Report of the High Level Panel of Experts on Food Security and Nutrition of the Committee on World Food Security*. Rome.

IPCC. 2015. *Meeting Report of the Intergovernmental Panel on Climate Change Expert Meeting on Climate Change, Food and Agriculture*. Dublin, Ireland and Geneva: World Meteorological Organisation.

Klumper, W. and Qaim, M. 2014. A Meta-Analysis of the Impacts of Genetically Modefied Crops. *PLOS ONE*, 9, 1–7.

Koizumi, T. 2015. Biofuels and Food Security. *Renewable and Sustainable Energy Reviews*, 50, 829–841.

Liversage, H. 2011. *Responding to 'Land Grabbing' and Promoting Responsible Investment in Agriculture*. Rome: IFAD

Malthus, T. R. 1798. *An Essay on the Principle of Population*. London: J. Johnson.

Mastrandrea, M. D., Mach, K. J., Plattner, G-K., Edenhofer, O., Stocker, T. F., Field, C. B., Ebi, K. L. and Matschoss, P. R. 2011. The IPCC AR5 Guidance Note on Consistent Treatment of Uncertainties: A Common Approach Across the Working Groups. *Climatic Change*, 108, 675–691.

McCorriston, S., Hemming, D. J., Lamontagne-Godwin, J. D., Osborn, J., Parr, M. J. and Roberts, P. D. 2013. *What Is the Evidence of the Impact of Trade Liberalisation on Food Security in Developing Countries? A Systematic Review*. London: EPPI-Centre, Social Science Research Unit, Institute of Education, University of London.

McIntyre, B. D., Herren, H. R., Wakhungu, J. and Watson, R. T. (eds.) 2009. *Agriculture at a Crossroads: Global Report*. Washington, DC: International Assessment of Agricultural Knowledge, Science and Technology for Development.

Millenium Ecosystem Assessment. 2005. *Ecosystems and Human Well-Being: Synthesis*. Washington, DC: Island Press

Negash, M. and Swinnen, J. 2013. Biofuels and Food Security: Micro-Evidence From Ethiopia. *Energy Policy*, 61, 963–976.

Nguyen, Q., Boyer, J., Howe, J., Bratkovich, S., Groot, H., Pepke, E. and Fernholz, K. 2017. *Global Production of Second Generation Biofuels: Trends and Influences*. Minneapolis: Dovetail Partners Inc.

Paillard, S., Treyer, S. and Dorin, B. (eds.) 2014. *AGRIMONDE: Scenarios and Challenges for Feeding the World in 2050*. Paris: Editions Quae.

Popkin, B. M. 1993. Nutritional Patterns and Transitions. *Population and Development Review*, 19, 138–157.

Popkin, B. M. 2001. The Nutrition Transition and Obesity in the Developing World. *The Journal of Nutrition*, 131, 8715–8735.

Popkin, B. M., Adair, L. S. and Ng, S. W. 2012. The Global Nutrition Transition: The Pandemic of Obesity in Developing Countries. *Nutrition Reviews*, 70, 3–21.

Porter, J. R., Chalinor, A. J., Cochrane, K., Howden, S. M., Iqbal, M. M., Lobell, D. B. and Travasso, M. I. 2014. Chapter 7: Food Security and Food Production Systems. *In:* IPCC (ed.) *Climate Change 2014: Impacts Adaptation and Vulnerability. Part A: Global and Sectoral Aspects: Contribution of Working Group II to the Fifth Assessment Report of the Intergovernmental Panel on Climate Change*. Cambridge and New York: Cambridge University Press.

Reilly, M. and Willenbockel, D. 2010. Managing Uncertainty: A Review of Food System Scenario Analysis and Modelling. *Philosophical Transactions of the Royal Society B-Biological Sciences*, 365, 3049–3063.

Sadras, V., Cassman, K., Grassini, P., Hall, A., Bastiaanssen, W., Laborte, A., Ae, M., Sileshi, G. and Steduto, P. 2015. *Yield Gap Analysis of Field Crops: Methods and Case Studies*. Rome: FAO and DWFI.

Saunois, M., Jackson, R. B., Bousquet, P., Poulter, B. and Canadell, J. G. 2016. The Growing Role of Methane in Antrhopogenic Climate Change. *Environmental Research Letters*, 11, 1–5.

Sen, A. 1981. *Poverty and Famines: An Essay on Entitlement and Deprivation*. Oxford: Clarendon Press.

Simon, J. L. 1977. *The Economics of Population Growth*. Princeton, NJ: Princeton University Press.

Simon, J. L. 1981. *The Ultimate Resource*. Princeton, NJ: Princeton University Press.

Simon, J. L. 1986. *Theory of Population and Economic Growth*. Oxford: Basil Blackwell.

Sims, R. E. H., Mabee, W., Saddler, J. N. and Taylor, M. 2010. An Overview of Second Generation Biofuel Technologies. *Bioresource Technology*, 101, 1570–1580.

Smil, V. 2002. Nitrogen and Food Production: Proteins and Human Diets. *Ambio*, 31, 6.

Su, Y., Zhang, P. and Su, Y. 2015. An Overview of Biofuels Policies and Industrialisation in the Major Biofuels Producing Countries. *Renewable and Sustainable Energy Reviews*, 50, 991–1003.

Sumner, D. A., Alston, J. M. and Glauber, J. W. 2010. Evolution of the Economics of Agricultural Policy. *American Journal of Agricultural Economics*, 92, 403–423.

UNCTAD. 2016. *Second Generation Biofuel Markets: State of Play, Trade and Developing Country Perspectives*. Geneva: UNCTAD/DITC/TED/2015/18.

United Nations. 2009. *World Population Prospects: The 2008 Revision*. New York: United Nations.

United Nations. 2011. *World Population Prospects: The 2010 Revision*. New York: United Nations.

United Nations. 2013. *World Population Prospects: The 2012 Revision*. New York: United Nations.

United Nations. 2015. *World Population Prospects: The 2015 Revision*. New York: United Nations.

US Geological Survey. 2016. *Mineral Commodity Summaries 2016*. Washington, DC: US Department of the Interior.

Von Braun, J. and Meinzen-Dick, R. 2009. "Land Grabbing" by Foreign Investors in Developing Countries: Risks and Opportunities. *IFPRI Policy Brief 13*.

Wiggins, S., Henley, G. and Keats, S. 2015. *Competitive or Complementary? Industrial Crops and Food Security in Sub-Saharan Africa*. London: Overseas Development Institute.

4 Food affordability, entitlements and poverty traps

Introduction

While the adequacy of food availability in relation to food needs will always remain a basic measure of food security, access to affordable food, the second dimension of food security is now recognised as a major factor governing the ability of individuals to feed themselves and their dependents. According to Sen (1981b), individuals have sufficient food to eat when their market exchange entitlements allow them to obtain enough food to satisfy their food requirements. This means that the focus is on individuals 'having sufficient food to eat' rather than there 'being sufficient food available' in a region or country. This marked the start of a shift away from the so-called 'food first' approach that, to a significant extent, continues to dominate policy debates on food security in many situations.

Market exchange entitlements represent the capacity of an individual or a household to produce or purchase food based on land and other resources available for food production, income from employment to purchase food in markets and any benefits in cash or kind from social security or private charity. This encourages a switch in attention from the performance of the food production and distribution system to the livelihoods of individuals and to the way in which these livelihoods are influenced by agricultural production, by broader economic activities, and by policies for social security safety nets and poverty alleviation.

The next section of this chapter summarises the exchange entitlement approach to the analysis of food security introduced by Sen, emphasising the potential influences of food production, and employment opportunities. In the third section, arguments from the literature on the dynamics of livelihoods and poverty are then reviewed and used to inform discussion and analysis of the dynamics of food security and the likely emergence of 'poverty traps'. The fourth and final section summarises the arguments and examines implications for policy intervention.

Access to affordable food: market exchange entitlements

Sen (1980, 1981b, 1981a, 1982) introduced the notion of 'market exchange entitlements' as the primary determinant of who is hungry and who is not. This was in opposition to the prevailing notion that hunger was a direct result of food scarcity and that the solution to problems of hunger and food insecurity was to ensure that sufficient food was produced and was available for consumption. What Sen proposed was that hunger arose, not because of a reduction in how much food was available in a particular country or region, but because some individuals or groups of individuals could not afford to consume sufficient food even if there was no actual physical scarcity of food, or food deficit. What mattered was the ability of individuals and households to establish a claim or 'entitlement' over the food they needed. This claim could be established in two main ways, either by producing the food required using their basic endowment of land, labour skills and other resources, or by using their resource endowment to purchase the necessary food from others, for example, in exchange for the proceeds from employment or from other economic activity. A third source of entitlements was through direct transfers from the state or other individuals as social security payments, aid or charity (Osmani, 1993). The overall implication of this approach is that hunger and famine arise due to entitlement failure. This can happen through production system failure (for example, because of a natural or weather-related calamity) or through resource endowment loss (for example, because of problems in the labour market through loss of employment or reduction in wages). It can also happen through exchange failure (for example, following a significant increase in the relative price of food) or through failure to secure sufficient transfer of resources from government programmes or private charity.

This approach broadens the focus of the analysis of food insecurity from an almost exclusive focus on problems associated with food production and food availability to a more general concern for hungry individuals and the various ways in which they might acquire the food they need and to the wide variety of ways in which this ability might be compromised. For example, natural disasters such as droughts, floods etc. would clearly lead to production failure and might also impact on employment and labour markets leading to endowment loss. War and civil disruption might lead to both production failure and endowment loss. In fact, Sen (2002) has emphasised that the continuing problem of widespread hunger in the world is primarily related to poverty and must be seen as being embedded in the larger issues of poverty and deprivation. In addition, this approach can also provide insights into the problems that arise when a section of society is excluded from the benefits of more general prosperity. In particular, where there is general economic growth including inflationary pressures, excluding a particular group from the benefits of growth could mean that they are priced out of the market unable to afford sufficient food; a case of exchange failure for this group.

Empirical evidence

Sen supported his views with detailed analysis of data from a number of famines in Africa and Asia; Bengal, 1943; Ethiopia, 1972–74; Sahel, 1968–73; and Bangladesh, 1974. In each case, he could show that, even if drought or flooding or other natural event led to a reduction in food availability, the direct impact of this initial shock on food availability and prices was generally quite limited. Even in the total absence of any significant impact on food availability, the main impact on food consumption of individuals and groups arose out of an impact on the livelihoods of people. And further evidence from more recent famines provides additional support for this approach, including the so-called free market famine in Niger in 2005. We summarise some of this evidence in the remainder of this section.

The Bengali famine 1943: In the case of the Bengali famine (1943) the initial trigger has been identified as the inflationary pressures arising from wartime expenditures. This meant that those who benefited from these expenditures were in a better position to purchase food and these people lived in the main urban areas. However, this on its own did not generate a major scarcity of food or a major increase in food prices. There were also a number of other changes, each individually quite minor but the cumulative effect was important. These changes included a small reduction in the winter rice crop arising through weather and disease over part of the crop, and the absence of imports from Burma after the Japanese invasion of that country. In addition, imports from other Indian states were prohibited as part of the wartime management of food supplies, and some speculation and panic purchasing had been precipitated by administrative confusion about the introduction and suspension of a Bengali state purchasing scheme.

One significant result of these changes was a substantial rise in the price of rice. Because people in rural areas did not benefit from the general rise in prosperity associated with the wartime expenditure, particularly those dependent either directly or indirectly on agriculture, one side effect of this price inflation was a significant reduction in real incomes. Agricultural labourers without the benefit of land on which to grow their own food were particularly badly hit. Considering the increase in food prices, the 'exchange rate' between agricultural labour and food grains (a measure of the ability of agricultural workers to purchase food) fell from a baseline of 100 in 1939-40 to around 30 in 1943-44. In fact, it was below 30 for significant periods during this time, reducing the purchasing power of agricultural workers to less than one third of what it had been. Rural artisans (shoemakers, carpenters etc.) were also badly hit, as well as those who supplied 'luxury' items such as, haircuts, bamboo umbrellas, dairy products, and fish, so the ability of these workers to purchase food was also severely impaired.

The fact that the famine most severely affected agricultural labourers, rural artisans, fishermen and providers of 'luxury' products such as milk and dairy products, while peasants and share-croppers were much less affected, is fully consistent with the exchange entitlements approach. In this situation, hunger and starvation for large numbers of individuals was the result of indirect effects of the initial impact on food prices, operating through supply and demand in food markets and other related markets, impacting on the livelihoods of agricultural labourers and livelihoods of the other rural workers that depended on them. The outcome was a severe reduction in their ability to purchase food or any other goods, resulting in widespread starvation.

The Ethiopian famine 1972–74: The famine in Ethiopia in 1972–74 began with an initial reduction in food availability triggered by the failure of rains in late 1972 and early 1973. The resulting crop and pasture failures reduced both food availability and the incomes of the agriculturalists and pastoralists in the area affected, with evidence of hunger and food shortage from late 1972, mainly in the

North-East (Wollo Province). The collapse in local incomes meant that those who were hungry could not generate an effective demand that would attract food from elsewhere in Ethiopia. This entitlement collapse (rather than alternative explanations based on transport bottlenecks) is consistent with the observed trajectory of market prices that increased only slightly during this period, and with the fact that some food continued to be exported from the region to the urban areas of Addis Ababa and Asmara.

However, Sen stresses that there we two distinct sets of direct victims to the Ethiopian famine: the farmers in the north-eastern Wollo Province, and the pastoralists in both Wollo and the southern province of Harerghe.

The Wollo farmers suffered a production failure as the crops on which they depended, both for food and for marketed surplus, failed because of the drought. At the same time, their ability to use the standard coping processes through selling assets (mainly land and livestock) was severely impaired by significant declines (some would say collapse) in both land and livestock prices. However, there was also a very significant indirect effect of these problems, as farmers reacted to the collapse in their exchange entitlements by dismissing employees and servants and expelling both family and non-family dependents. The induced destitution of these groups meant a further collapse in the demand for food and, more importantly, exacerbated the decline in the demand for non-food goods and services in these areas. This had an additional knock-on impact on the incomes of those who supplied these goods and services (artisans and other service suppliers), leading to a collapse of the ability of these groups to maintain their food exchange entitlements and to the further spread of hunger and starvation.

The impact on pastoralists followed a similar pattern, though there were additional factors operating here. In addition to losses arising directly from drought, there were additional background difficulties arising from loss of key dry-season grazing lands as commercial agriculture expanded in the fertile river valley lands. An important result of these processes was the virtual collapse in the relative price of livestock versus that of grain, the livestock-grain exchange rate. This had serious implications for the ability of pastoralists to cope with the initial problems created by the drought. In the first place, grains are an indispensable low-cost source of calories for pastoralists, less than half the cost of calories from livestock products. This means that demand for grains would increase in times of difficulty such as those created by the drought. Secondly, the use of livestock as a store of wealth (as well as a source of income) meant that in times of difficulty, dissaving would be a normal coping strategy. The increased sale of livestock would lead to a reduction in prices, further exacerbated by the fact that many animals would be in poor and emaciated condition due to the effects of the drought. A third factor influencing the relative prices of grain and livestock in these circumstances is the fact that grain provides a much more flexible and divisible source of calories, introducing a further premium on grain prices.

In short, the trajectory of the Ethiopian famine is fully consistent with an explanation based on failure of entitlements, rather than a decline in food availability.

The famine in Niger in 2005: The famine in Niger in 2005 provides a more recent example of a situation where minor disruption of food supplies are amplified by resulting movements in market prices that undermined people's exchange entitlements and disrupted the livelihoods of thousands of individuals in a relatively limited area over a short period of time (Rubin, 2009; Rubin, 2016; Mousseau and Mittal, 2006).

Cereal production was disrupted by a drought, and there was further disruption to available pasture when a locust swarm invaded the area in the latter half of 2004. At that stage, both USAID and the Famine Early Warning System Network (FEWSNET) estimated that national cereal production was reduced by approximately 11 per cent below the average of the previous five years and that the food deficit could be covered by a three per cent increase in normal cereal imports. This led them to describe the situation in Niger, not as a 'famine' but as a 'very severe but localised food crisis', prompting a muted response from the national government and international aid agencies. This meant that a limited amount of cereals was made available at subsidised prices, rather than the targeted distribution of free food undertaken by other countries in the region. This intervention proved totally inadequate and by early 2005 entitlements were beginning to collapse for a large proportion of families in the affected area. Cereal prices had more than doubled in this period while livestock prices were reduced by half, so that the purchasing power of livestock dependent households were less than a quarter of what it had been before the crisis. This meant that most hungry households could not afford even the limited amount of subsidised food made available by government and aid agencies and led to tens of thousands of deaths among adults and children.

This is one example of where relying on food availability indicators led international agencies, including USAID and FEWSNET, to determine that the situation in Niger in 2005 was no more than a localised severe food crisis. This seriously dampened and curtailed the response of the international community and the provision of food aid that, in retrospect, was badly needed and would likely have prevented the deaths of tens of thousands of individuals. The Nigerien government's response, making limited amounts of food available in the markets at subsidised prices, proved entirely inadequate. The government believed that large amounts of free aid would interfere with the stability of markets, increase dependency and hamper attempts to find a long-run solution; this attitude has led some commentators to refer to the Nigerien 2005 famine as the 'free market famine'. It is not possible to judge whether a more detailed consideration of the situation of individuals in the area, such as would have been facilitated by using the entitlements approach, would have led to a different outcome. However, by focusing on the livelihoods of individuals and families, using the entitlements framework could have had a significant advantage over the food availability approach by prompting a more targeted approach to famine and hunger relief such as that adopted, with significantly more success, by other countries in the region at that time.

Summary and critique

Sen emphasises the continuing importance of food availability and the complex relationship between changes in human population and changes in food production. He goes on to argue that this must not be allowed to obscure the important role played by the labour market and rural markets more generally; these underpin the economic viability of rural households and in particular their role in providing an adequate and consistent supply of food for the family. These markets also encompass sales of assets, especially sales of land and livestock. Those who sell assets in response to hard times are mostly small landholders and small herders, and while these sales may provide relief from current difficulties by allowing immediate food purchases, they will usually lead to an increase in the vulnerability of the family and household in the longer run. In this context, dynamic aspects related to the evolution of rural livelihoods and the potential emergence of poverty traps are discussed in more detail in the next section of this chapter.

In the famines examined here, there were significant impacts on all groups of people who rely on rural markets to provide their entitlements to food. These include the sellers of agricultural inputs and also the sellers of services and other non-agricultural items regularly used as part of daily living by rural families: barbers, beer sellers, craftsmen etc. The incomes of these groups of people and their ability to construct entitlements that give them command over sufficient food to avoid hunger and famine remain vulnerable to changes in the incomes of other participants in the rural economy. Sen (1987) also emphasises that the issues arising in the case of famine (as outlined and discussed above) parallel those that arise in the case of chronic undernourishment and hunger and have similar implications for policy intervention.

Summary: To help summarise the entitlement approach, Figure 4.1 provides a framework for illustrating and analysing the principal variables and their relationships to market exchange entitlements and food affordability. Here, we use a simplified, four-quadrant diagram. The axes represent, firstly, the endowment available to an individual or a group and how this endowment is allocated between food production (P) and food purchases (M), and, secondly, the amount of food entitlement arising from production (Fp) and from purchase (Fm). The top right-hand (north-eastern) quadrant of the diagram allows a comparison between exogenously determined food requirements with the level of food entitlement. This latter arises from decisions about how a given endowment of resources is allocated between food production (represented by the production function in the top left-hand quadrant of the diagram) and food purchasing (represented by the food price line in the bottom right quadrant of the diagram).

The endowment of the individual (or group) is represented by the 45-degree Endowment Line in the lower left-hand (south-western) quadrant; the distance of this line from origin represents the level of resources available including the aggregate rental value of land and equipment available for food production and the earning capacity of labour resources. Changes in this endowment are represented by movements of the line towards origin (reductions) or away from origin (increases).

Changes in production efficiency and productivity, on the other hand, are represented by changes in the slope of the Food Production Function in the top left-hand (north-western) quadrant, downwards for productivity reductions and upwards for productivity increases. Similarly, the slope of the Food Price Line in

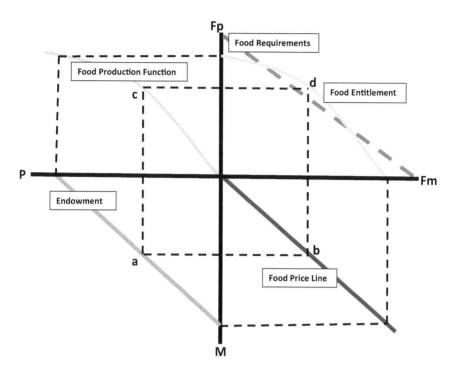

Figure 4.1 A simple illustration of the entitlements approach to food affordability

the lower right-hand (south-eastern) quadrant represents the market price of food, pivoting to the right to represent a reduction in price and to the left to represent a price increase.

Point 'a' on the Endowment Line in the south-western quadrant represents one possible allocation of resources between food production and food purchase, supporting a combination of food purchases at point 'b' on the Food Price Line in the south-eastern quadrant and food production at point 'c' on the Food Production Function in the north-western quadrant. This combination of production and purchase supports total food entitlement at point 'd' on the Food Entitlement Line in the north-eastern quadrant. Other points on the Food Entitlement Line can be attained, at least in principle, by other allocations of the available endowment of assets between production and purchase. For food producers, some part of this endowment will comprise resources such as land, livestock and farm equipment. While in principle, these assets can be sold or rented out to allow an individual or household to purchase food in the short term, the sale of these assets can seriously compromise longer-term food entitlements.

Food needs, determined by per capita requirements and levels of population, affluence and urbanisation as discussed in Chapter 3, are represented by the Food Requirements Line in the north-eastern quadrant. Changes can be illustrated by shifts in this line, upwards to the right for increases, downwards to the left for decreases.

The pattern of exchange entitlements explored here is firmly focused on the functioning of a market economy. This allows individuals to exchange their endowment of resources (most simply labour power and skills, but can also include markets for land, livestock and other assets) for money income that can then be used to obtain entitlement to the food they need for their own use and the use of their families and other dependents. Hunger, starvation and famine are the inevitable outcomes when there is failure to obtain sufficient of these entitlements. However, this analysis implies that income is only one factor among a range of factors that need to be considered. Income depends on the assets commanded by individuals and families, so rather than starting the analysis with income levels it is important to move the focus back at least to the stage of asset endowments. This suggests a hierarchy in the analyses. For example, the presence of hunger and starvation might prompt us to ask why people are hungry. If we then discover that people do not have enough income to purchase the food they need, we must also question why they do not have sufficient income, and even raise questions about why they do not have sufficient assets to command the income to purchase the food they need to avoid hunger. Clearly the hierarchy of analyses does not stop there, because behind the asset endowments of individuals and families lie issues of inheritance, educational opportunities, savings and investment opportunities and even employment opportunities in the past. In fact, we might legitimately question the whole structure of economic and social institutions in the search for the causes of hunger and starvation.

Yet the role of markets remains a primary factor in both causing and relieving hunger and the efficiency of markets is often quoted as a reason for not instituting 'intrusive' interventions to relieve the worst cases. As Sen points out, this is in fact a misunderstanding of the standard arguments of market efficiency, for example, those presented in the original analysis by Adam Smith. These arguments are about the efficiency of free markets in meeting an existing demand (for food or any other good or service). They have nothing to say about situations where there is a clear need, but where this need does not get translated into an effective market demand.

The failure to translate food needs into effective demand is illustrated by the continuing export of food from famine-stricken areas that has been observed in a wide range of circumstances. According to the Food Availability Decline (FAD) model of famines, the onset of a reduction in food availability would result in a rise in food prices, which would then attract food from other areas and countries as merchants sought to take advantage of the higher prices to make profits. The analysis of the exchange entitlements of individuals and groups in the region clearly shows that this will be an inadequate approach, since those who are hungry will not be able to purchase the food that they need. In fact, famine areas will suffer a decline in effective food demand, often accompanied by a decline in food prices. This means that trade in food is quite likely to move out of the area rather than into the area, as observed in a wide range of famine situations where this type of naïve free-market philosophy has dominated decision making. This remains a problem, though with less dramatic consequences, in many areas affected by chronic hunger.

A related issue of current interest, is the potential impact on individual and household incomes, and hence on market exchange entitlements, of increased openness to trade arising from pursuit of the globalisation agenda. While there is evidence that incomes in developing countries gain from increased openness to trade, evidence of income gains in developing countries is more mixed (Kim, 2011). Moreover, the impact of increased openness to trade on food security per se is ambiguous. McCorriston et al. (2013) examined the results of 34 studies that focused on agricultural trade liberalisation and food security and found no consistent conclusions. While 13 of the 34 studies found that food security would improve, ten reported a decline, while the remaining 11 reported mixed outcomes with variations across groups of people, regions and time periods or with alternative food security measures suggesting different outcomes for individual countries. The authors suggest that this lack of clear evidence is primarily attributable to difficulties in isolating the impact of trade liberalisation from the effects of the other policy changes implemented as part of a liberalisation package. At the same time, recent experience with trade and food security following the 2008 food price spike would support the notion that any attempts to isolate domestic food markets from international markets are likely to have negative effects and will, in most instances, be counterproductive (Gillson and Fouad, 2015). While increased openness to trade can have significant benefits, FAO (2015) points out that the trade liberalisation process must be carefully managed to ensure that positive impacts on food security outweigh the negative impacts.

Critique: There have been many critical assessments of the entitlement approach. These have focused on a range of issues including Sen's (mis)interpretation and analysis of the data from the specific famines that he analysed. His selection of those particular famines rather than other specific famines has also been criticised. Other criticisms have focused on issues related to the theoretical contribution of the entitlement approach and its ability to encompass all salient aspects of contemporary famines and chronic hunger.

For example, one group of authors (including Bowbrick (1986), Devereux (1988)) focused on the specific famines analysed by Sen and suggested that his use of data, for example, that discussed in the previous sections of this chapter, tended to underestimate the contribution of food availability decline to these famines, tending to exaggerate the importance of exchange entitlement failure.

Another group of authors focused on a number of famines that were not analysed by Sen and set out to show that focusing only on the collapse of exchange entitlements tended to undermine the clear significance of decline in food production and availability as the principal trigger for famines. Kula (1988) and Nolan (1993) looked at the famine generally associated with the Chinese Great Leap Forward, and Baulch (1987) examined the 1980s famine in Northern Ethiopia.

However, Devereux (2001) suggested that these lines of criticism are misdirected. They are focused on the assumption that food availability decline is an independent alternative hypothesis to exchange entitlements decline as a causal factor in famines. It is clear from Sen's writings and that of other commentators (for example, Osmani (1993)) that this is not the case. In fact, the exchange entitlement approach and framework already incorporates food availability decline as one of the factors that leads to entitlement failure, seeing it as part of the failure of direct entitlements and production failure. Devereux suggests that the mechanisms through which entitlement failure arises vary from place to place and time to time. Thus, some famines may be triggered by production failure and direct entitlement failure (i.e. by Food Availability Decline), while others are mainly the result of exchange failure even while food availability remains at adequate levels. He sees a third group of famines triggered mainly by political failures where government policies, conflict and war are the main triggers of entitlement failure for specific groups of people.

Devereux goes on to suggest that the entitlement approach does not fully accommodate circumstances where households voluntarily limit their consumption to levels below that necessary to sustain the health and lives of all individuals in the household. This may be a response to the onset of hunger, especially when the expectation is that this hunger is likely to be a temporary phenomenon. It has been observed and described as part of the early stages of a more complex coping mechanism in a number of studies such as those by Corbett (1988), Cutler (1984) and Watts (1983). This can be a viable strategy that is focused on not impairing future productive capacity by choosing to consume less in the current period when food is scarce and expensive. The overriding objective is the avoidance of asset depletion rather than maintaining consumption levels. This can be interpreted as consistent with the entitlement approach when a dynamic view is taken and entitlements are viewed as multi-period intertemporal entitlement sets. However, Devereux points out that even this extension of the concept cannot explain the well-documented cases of situations where mortality in a family or group coexists with unrealised entitlements, where members of the household are dying even when the household retains assets that it could exchange for food.

More recent analysis and debate (Rubin, 2016) reiterates many of these criticisms, emphasising the continuing danger of overlooking the importance of food supply by focusing on the impact of entitlement failure on food demand. This analysis also emphasises the need to ensure that individual needs are reflected in the market demand for food. Yet Rubin acknowledges the advantage for the analysis and understanding of chronic hunger, of using a framework that focuses on the relationship between food and individuals, rather than focusing on aggregate food availability at regional or country level. Rubin also emphasises the difficulties faced by the entitlement approach in dealing comprehensively with the impact of wars and societal collapse on vulnerability to hunger and famine and the failure to provide a framework for analysing the political dimensions of situations where hunger and famine are used as a military or political weapon.

Despite these persistent problems, the entitlement approach is widely used to analyse both famine episodes and ongoing chronic hunger. Consumption rationing can be interpreted as part of a dynamic coping response to entitlement problems. In addition, even with additional complexities arising from the political instability and civil conflict, much of the impact of war and conflict on hunger and famine can also be analysed within the entitlement framework.

The fact that income is not the only factor influencing hunger has been further emphasised by recent experiences with the Millennium Development Goals. In particular, the resounding success in reducing the proportion of people suffering from extreme poverty, from 47 per cent in 1990 to 14 per cent in 2015, is contrasted with the more modest achievements in reducing the proportion of people suffering hunger, from 23 per cent in 1990 to 13 per cent in 2015 (United Nations, 2015). While these gains can undoubtedly be attributed to significant economic growth over this period, it is acknowledged that persistent and pernicious inequalities remain, as millions of people are being left behind. These marginalised people will include those who are among the poorest and those at particular disadvantage because of their sex, age, disability, ethnicity or geographic location. For example, von Braun et al. (2009) focus on the social and economic exclusion of groups of people as an important characteristic of those who suffer from hunger and starvation. The study points in particular to indigenous peoples, to groups regarded as socially or politically inferior, to people living in remote areas and to minority groups, where participation in economic activity and political decision making is curtailed. Many of these groups are often significantly over-represented among those suffering from food insecurity. The study marks an important shift in the focus for studies of poverty and hunger by highlighting the varied experiences of different groups of poor people under the continuing efforts by governments and international agencies to relieve poverty and hunger.

More recently, Hickey and du Toit (2013) have pointed out that while social exclusion will likely place groups of people at a disadvantage and promote chronic poverty (and hunger), there are many situations where a group that is not excluded in any real sense can still be significantly disadvantaged in gaining access to economic and social assets and political power. This can be described as a case of adverse incorporation, where participation in social, economic and political activities is subject to discriminatory rules, norms and practices that severely limit the advantages that can be achieved through the group's participation.

Livelihood dynamics and poverty traps

The principal implication of the entitlements approach is that changes in the livelihoods of vulnerable individuals, in their poverty level and in their ability to purchase food are more important in the onset and evolution of hunger and famine than change in food availability. In this section of the chapter, we look more closely at patterns of livelihood change and, in particular, at the range of circumstances that impair the ability of households and individuals to continue improving the resources, skills and productivity that support improvements in wellbeing and nutrition. These circumstances appear to trap individuals and households in a situation where their levels of resources and skills lead to persistent poverty and chronic hunger, presenting the ultimate challenge to policy makers who would design and implement interventions to eliminate these problems. For this reason we investigate the mechanisms through which these poverty traps might arise, we critically examine the evidence for these traps in a variety of settings, and we consider the implications for interventions that focus on the relief or elimination of poverty and hunger.

Mechanisms and evidence for poverty traps

This particular problem of non-convergence between the economic prosperity of countries regions and groups of individuals, often attributed to 'poverty traps', has been widely investigated. A range of explanations for the persistence of poverty and hunger has been identified. Here we focus on the circumstances in which individuals and households might be trapped at low levels of prosperity and wellbeing.

Exploring poverty trap mechanisms: A variety of mechanisms have been proposed as the basis for different types of poverty traps (Kraay and McKenzie, 2014). These include mechanisms that can generate traps that arise at the level of the whole macro-economy, those that operate at an individual or household level and those that relate to traps arising in a single geographic area.

Poverty traps can arise from mechanisms operating across the whole economy because of problems related to the overall level of savings or because of issues related to coordinating private investments and complementary investment in social and commercial infrastructure, such as that related to health and education systems, transport and communications.

A number of mechanisms relate to traps at the level of a single individual or household. These include nutrition-based poverty traps that arise when a person's earnings fall to levels that are insufficient to provide the minimum calories needed to maintain health and productivity. This reduction in earnings can trigger a downward spiral as earning capacity is progressively impaired by the health problems arising from the initial fall in nutrition levels. Another proposed mechanism affecting individuals and households is related to the presence of restrictions on borrowing when there is a need for lumpy investments to improve productivity and earning capacity. These may involve investments in education or personal health that improve skills and productivity or may involve business-related investment in facilities and equipment. A trap arises whenever borrowing levels are restricted by the person's current low earning capacity and asset endowment, thus blocking further improvement in earning capacity or asset levels.

Kraay and McKenzie (2014) also consider poverty traps arising from the behaviour of individuals. These suggest that poverty may be self-reinforcing because of the way in which it affects decision making, reducing the propensity for reinvestment that would facilitate growth out of poverty. In addition, they explore geographic poverty traps arising from lack of resources and infrastructure in a remote area that tightly constrains the productivity of individual skills and household resources so that earning capacity and wellbeing cannot increase sufficiently over time to support an escape from poverty.

Bowles et al. (2006) provide an alternative classification of these mechanisms involving three broad categories. One category concerns the existence of critical thresholds. These are defined in terms of individual wealth or human capital and may be measured at individual level, in terms of a minimum level of nutrition, or a minimum level of skills or productivity to enable sustainable participation in economic activity. These thresholds may also be measured at a regional or national level, in terms of minimum investments needed to provide the educational, transport and communications infrastructure to support the continuing productivity of individual workers. Taken together, this means that the thresholds faced by individuals depend on the levels of regional or national investment in infrastructure. With low levels of investment in education and training, or with poor and inefficient transport infrastructure, a poor farmer may never be able to save enough to enhance skills and productivity sufficiently to escape poverty and hunger.

A second category looks at the institutions in society and the extent to which these can inhibit individual and collective growth in prosperity in ways that trap individuals in poverty and hunger. Examples of this type of dysfunctional institutional structure include those that might arise in a highly unequal society so that there is little political support for investment in public education or in the wide-ranging protection of property rights across a broad section of society. In these circumstances, the lack of well-protected property rights will inhibit levels of investment and reduce overall income levels, while the lack of a broad-based system of public education will likely lead to the emergence of groups with low levels of skills, achievements and incomes. More extreme examples of institutional deficiencies that can generate hunger/poverty traps could arise where the government is kleptocratic or where health services are poorly developed so that life expectancy is low. In all these cases, incentives to invest in productive activities will be curtailed leading to persistently lower levels of prosperity and incomes.

The third category is focused on the potential impact of neighbourhood effects arising from an individual's membership of different groups. These include those that are fixed (such as ethnicity or race), as well as those that result from individual decisions (such as area of residence or schools attended). The interaction between the decisions made by individuals and the reaction of other group members can have a significant effect on the outcome of these decisions.

Yet another classification of poverty trap mechanisms is provided by Barrett and Carter (2013), for whom the key distinction is between poverty traps that can be represented by a model that involves a single economic equilibrium and those that are more appropriately represented using a model with more than one equilibrium.

Individuals facing a single economic equilibrium are unambiguously poor and do not have access to sufficient skills, capital or infrastructure to escape from poverty and hunger. Moreover, the incentives they face discourage them from any efforts or investments that would lead to self-improvement, and there is no possibility of making things better through any feasible action on their part. These circumstances can arise when there are problems with market and institutional arrangements governing incentives, when there are severe geographic disadvantages and/or when available technology is not sufficiently productive to provide a livelihood free from hunger and poverty. These problems may also occur for individuals suffering from severe mental or physical disabilities. For groups of individuals, they may arise from discrimination, other forms of adverse incorporation, or social exclusion.

Multiple equilibrium poverty traps arise when individuals or groups face a threshold level of skills, resources and earning capacity that determines whether they are on an upward trajectory to a sustainable livelihood that provides freedom from hunger and poverty or whether they are constrained to a livelihood that can provide only a low level of wellbeing characterised by hunger and poverty. As illustrated in Figure 4.2, this threshold marks a tipping point in earning capacity, labelled E^0_t. With earning capacity above this level, the individual or group has incentives to save and to invest in additional skills and resources, allowing expansion of earning capacity to reach the higher sustainable equilibrium income level, E^H_t. Starting with earning capacity below E^0_t, these incentives do not exist; instead of expanding, earning capacity is reduced, for example, through the sale of productive assets in order to purchase sufficient food to ensure survival. This means that the individual or household converges on the lower income level, E^L_t, and is trapped at this low level of household and family welfare, since there is no systematic way of escaping. These circumstances can arise where a minimum level of capital is required to undertake the necessary investments, and the individual does not have access to savings or borrowing facilities to meet this capital requirement. These circumstances may also arise when social investment in education, health, transport and communication infrastructure is not sufficient to allow development of the necessary skills or accumulation of the necessary level of savings.

The diagram illustrates the relationship between earning capacity of an individual or group of individuals in two successive time periods (E_t, E_{t+1}), showing how available incentives influence the evolution of livelihoods. The Sustainability Frontier represents the evolutionary path where livelihoods are non-declining, having the same value in each of the two periods; this is considered 'just sustainable'

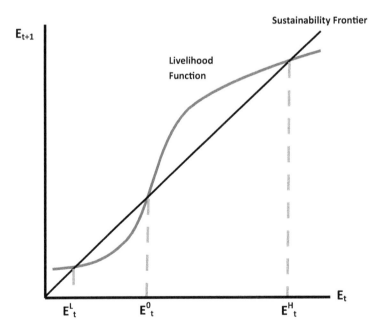

Figure 4.2   A simple illustration of a threshold scenario leading to a poverty trap

according to conventional definitions of sustainability (Arrow et al., 2003). The Livelihood Function illustrates a typical trajectory of earning capacity for a particular individual or group. As noted in the discussion above, a key feature of this function is the existence of a threshold, E^0_t. Skills and resources that provide an earning capacity above this level in the initial period are required in order to establish a sustainable income trajectory, where income does not decline over time. Only in these circumstances will there be sufficient incentives to take the steps needed to increase earning capacity over time.

Increases in the level of human and physical capital commanded by an individual can be represented by a shift upwards and to the left of the Livelihood Function, while increases in the productivity of existing human and physical capital can be represented by increase in the slope. Institutional and neighbourhood effects can be represented by shifts to the right in the Livelihood Function, increasing the threshold level of earnings capacity needed to break the poverty trap and likely reducing both the higher and the lower equilibrium income levels.

Testing the evidence for poverty traps: Kraay and McKenzie (2014) investigate broad evidence for country-level poverty traps by examining changes in per capita income. Lack of income growth and persistence of poverty over the long term would indicate the possible presence of this type of trap. They inspect data for real GDP per capita (adjusted for differences in purchasing power) for 110 countries. Over the 50 years, 1960–2010 they find no evidence of long-term stagnation of incomes. While some individual countries experience very low rates of growth or even decline in per capita GDP over these five decades, the data show that the poorest groups of countries (those in the two lowest quintiles of the initial income distribution) are growing at least as fast as those countries at the top of the initial income distribution. Even the poorest 10 per cent of countries show an average growth rate at around 1.8 per cent per year, similar to that of the United States over the last 200 years. They believe that this rate of growth is more than sufficient to ensure that, over 50 years, these countries will have grown out of any poverty trap by moving past any threshold or tipping point that might have been present.

Two key pieces of evidence for country-level poverty traps are not observed in the data. First of all, stagnant incomes are rarely observed, and when observed, are clearly not related to initial income levels. Secondly, there is no evidence that thresholds exist or any evidence of the predicted acceleration in growth rates when thresholds are crossed and poor countries emerge from a trap.

However, most theoretical models of poverty traps focus on individual households and on how incomes and household assets change from year to year. When a trap exists, households with low levels of income and assets that leave them below a given threshold tipping point find that they cannot save and invest enough to improve their prospects and, in the absence of outside assistance, find that they are locked into a downward spiral. At the same time, individuals with assets and income above the threshold tipping point have sufficient resources and positive incentives to pursue a strategy of savings and investment that ensures a continued high level of wellbeing and prosperity.

Barrett and Carter (2013) point out that the detailed household panel data needed to test for the existence of this type of poverty trap is not widely available. However, there have been a significant number of studies of these issues, providing mixed evidence about the possible existence of household level poverty traps. Kraay and McKenzie (2014) reviewed a selection of studies that examined year-to-year changes in household asset levels. These studies were searching for evidence that the evolution of asset levels over time was consistent with the existence of a threshold tipping point in decisions about savings and investment for these households. No evidence for this kind of poverty trap has been found in studies that involved households in China, Hungary, Russia, rural Pakistan and Ethiopia. By contrast, Barrett et al. (2006) find evidence for this type of poverty trap for rural households in Kenya and Madagascar, while Adato et al. (2006) find similar evidence among households in South Africa. More recently, You (2017), in a study of rural households in China, finds evidence of a dynamic asset threshold for the accumulation of agricultural assets; those with assets below this threshold are likely trapped in a regime of low levels of income in the long run.

Kraay and McKenzie (2014) also query the logic underlying some of the mechanisms (described above) that seek to explain the existence of poverty traps in specific circumstances. Of particular interest in this book is the possible existence of a nutrition-based poverty trap, such as that suggested by Dasgupta and Ray (1986). Persistent poverty can be self-reinforcing when hunger and malnourishment reduce a worker's productivity to the point where they are unable to earn enough income to provide sufficient calories to alleviate malnourishment, leading to a downward spiral in productivity and food entitlement. Kraay and McKenzie (2014) suggest that this well-known mechanism is untenable in the vast majority of circumstances. They point out that the food needed to maintain worker productivity and earning capacity is generally available for between 5 per cent and 25 per cent of daily wages, even for those in extreme poverty. They claim that this level of food entitlement would be available to all, except in the most extraordinary circumstances involving market breakdown and famine or in cases of severe gastro-enteritis disease.

In addition, Kraay and McKenzie query the logic underlying another well-known mechanism that may lead to trapping individuals in hunger and poverty. This mechanism, also discussed above, involves imperfect capital markets that place restrictive limits on borrowing by poor individuals in circumstances when they need significant start-up investments to improve their earning capacity. Thus, the individual is trapped at the lower level of income. However, Kraay and McKenzie point out that, while credit rationing and imperfect capital markets are widely acknowledged as problems, the specific impacts described are not readily defensible. In the first place, a person on low income usually has a wide range of options available for investment that may range in scale down to very low levels of required investment. In these circumstances, the problem of lumpy investment requirements disappears since, by choosing a suitable scale of investment, personal savings and family and other borrowing can overcome the problem of credit rationing.

There is thus no strong evidence to support the existence of many of the commonly proposed mechanisms that give rise to poverty traps. In particular, there is a distinct lack of evidence for mechanisms based on the existence of a threshold tipping point for an unconditional trajectory to adequate assets, income and nutrition. This would point to a cautious and sceptical approach to the need for a 'big push' policy of investments aimed at enabling individuals, households, regions and countries to climb past a threshold in assets, income or nutrition. Similar scepticism would be warranted about the prospects for this type of intervention in launching a self-sustaining pathway to adequate nutrition and prosperity.

However, some investigations, especially those focused on disadvantaged groups in remote rural areas, have provided positive evidence for the existence of multiple equilibrium poverty traps that involve threshold tipping points. In addition, the existence of this type of poverty trap might be easily masked by the admitted shortcomings in data availability and by a number of unresolved technical problems in econometric estimation. At the same time, the existence of single equilibrium traps has not been specifically investigated in any of the studies reported here, nor has there been any attempt to consider the possibility of traps that involve the simultaneous operation of more than one mechanism. Thus, we may conclude that the evidence indicates poverty traps may be rare, but it does not suggest that poverty traps do not still exist in some circumstances.

This means that the case for intervention to improve the assets, income and nutrition of individuals and groups subject to discrimination and social exclusion and for those living in remote and disadvantaged areas, still remains valid. Similarly, the case also remains for interventions to improve child and maternal nutrition, and for a wide variety of interventions to improve the assets and skills of poor individuals and households to enable them to escape poverty and hunger.

Summary and policy implications

This chapter considers the difference, highlighted by Sen, between an individual having sufficient food to eat and there being sufficient food available in a country or region. This encourages us to focus on the ability of individuals and families to achieve command over sufficient food and on the notion of market exchange entitlements. We consider three main sources of entitlements (production, market exchange, and direct transfers from state or private charity) and summarise some of the ways in which each of these may fail.

We review evidence from Sen and others on the emergence and trajectories of famines in the late 20th and early 21st centuries. In contrast to the traditional views of analysts and policy makers, this evidence points to the limited influence of reduced food availability in these famines and the importance of failure in rural markets, especially labour markets and the markets for productive assets such as land and livestock, and for specialist and craft services such as haircuts and bamboo umbrellas. The key message from this analysis is that reduced availability of food may be one of a number of changes that trigger a failure in food entitlements for one group of people (usually agricultural labourers or farmers with limited land). However, the reaction of rural markets to this initial change can lead to a reduction in entitlements for much larger and more diverse groups who also depend on rural markets for their livelihoods.

The principal implication of this switch is to highlight the importance of the livelihoods of individuals in the emergence, not only of famines, but also of less acute forms of transient and chronic hunger. This emphasises the need to consider these livelihoods, and their evolution over time, as a major focus for efforts to prevent and relieve famine and hunger. As well as short-term relief of hunger through direct food distribution and supplementary income payments, this analysis also points to the need for intermediate and longer-term interventions to enhance the livelihoods of individuals and families via education and training as well as policies that encourage entrepreneurship and investment in agriculture and other economic activities. However, since the problem derives from the inability of individuals to translate their need for food into an effective market demand for food, these interventions can only be successful if they are firmly focused on the needs of individuals, rather than, more generally, on the availability of food in the market.

The chapter also reviews a range of criticisms of the entitlements approach and the evidence that Sen analysed and presented in its support. These include those criticisms that dispute Sen's interpretation of the famines that he analysed, as well as criticisms that suggest he may have been overly selective in analysing those particular famine episodes. The general import of these studies is to suggest that the original analysis may have downplayed the influence of reductions in food availability and overemphasised the role of exchange entitlements failure in triggering these famines. However, the consensus appears to be that these criticisms are largely based on misinterpretations of the entitlements approach, arising from a failure to recognise that Sen is presenting both a general framework for the analyses of famines and a new theory about the cause of some famines in specific circumstances.

However, there are other criticisms acknowledged by Sen and his supporters. One such criticism highlights the fact that some individuals and families can engage in strict consumption rationing as a short-term coping mechanism for the onset of hunger and famine, reducing consumption below normal requirements so as to avoid disposal of key assets and enhance the chances for longer-term survival. Nevertheless, this scenario also is consistent with the entitlements approach when it can be extended to incorporate the notion of multi-period entitlements. The notion of extra-entitlement transfers arising from criminality, war, civil disturbance or political instability also creates problems for using the exchange entitlements approach in analysing famine episodes and hunger. However, it is clear that this approach can still be used to analyse much of the impact of war, conflict and civil disturbance on famine and hunger.

This chapter also considers the dynamic evolution of individual livelihoods and the factors that contribute to the emergence of poverty and hunger 'traps', where individuals are prevented from achieving adequate entitlements to food despite their best efforts. This analysis is particularly relevant in that it points to circumstances in which both individual coping mechanisms and policy interventions may fail.

However, there is no strong evidence to support the existence of many of the commonly proposed mechanisms that give rise to poverty traps, although some investigations provide evidence of poverty traps in the case of disadvantaged groups in remote rural areas. But significant gaps remain in the availability of data and in research on some mechanisms and combinations of mechanisms, as well as unresolved technical problems in econometric estimation.

This means that we can make a case for intervention to improve the assets, income and nutrition of individuals and groups subject to discrimination and social exclusion and for those living in remote and disadvantaged areas. Similarly, the case also remains for interventions to improve child and maternal nutrition and for a wide variety of interventions to improve the assets and skills of poor individuals and households to enable them to escape poverty and hunger.

A number of these interventions are briefly discussed in Fan et al. (2014). These authors first consider safety net programmes that focus on providing immediate relief for current problems (food transfers, supplementary feeding, food-for-work, food price subsidies and cash transfers). Secondly, they consider other approaches that are more concerned about longer-term impacts on individual livelihoods and focus on asset building, insurance and credit. Thirdly, they discuss policies that focus on infrastructure and the wider economy including trade policies, market information and infrastructure investment.

In considering the expansion of poverty eradication programmes in developing countries, Hanlon et al. (2010) point to increased popularity of cash transfer programmes. They focus in particular on the accumulating evidence that this approach to poverty alleviation provides an affordable and efficient means of supporting individual livelihoods, that is effective in relieving short-term problems related to hunger and generates longer-term impacts that relieve household vulnerability and can kick-start a virtuous cycle of investment and consumption at the household, community and national levels. However, they point out that many of these impacts are more likely delivered in programmes that provide a level of payment that is sufficient to make a difference to patterns of expenditure on food and other items and where the continuation of payments into the future is assured. In other words, a cash transfer programme that is designed to provide a short-term safety net is not likely to influence decisions about consumption patterns or investment. They also consider the ongoing debates about the extent to which these programmes should be targeted and whether payments should be conditional on specific activities by the recipients. They suggest that targeting is essential to ensure that payments reach those who are most likely to benefit, and while they agree that conditionality is often regarded as necessary for political acceptability, they point to clear evidence that unconditional cash transfers can provide significant benefits at much lower administrative costs.

A comprehensive evaluation of cash transfer programmes for both poverty reduction and social protection has been undertaken by Bastagli et al. (2016), taking advantage of the rapid expansion of the number and size of these programmes since the mid-1990s, as noted by Barrientos (2013). Bastagli et al. examine a wide range of programme evaluation studies over 15 years, 2000–2015, considering the impact on monetary poverty, education, employment, empowerment, health and nutrition, and savings, investment and production. The results are based on a review of 165 studies (chosen from an initial list of 201), covering 56 different pransfer programmes based in Latin America (54 per cent), Sub-Saharan Africa (38 per cent) and other developing countries (8 per cent). A large majority of the studies that examine monetary poverty show a statistically significant increase in total household expenditure as well as expenditure on food, and a significant decrease in at least one poverty measure. Almost all of the studies that focused on education show significant increases in cognitive development and a decrease in absenteeism, while those that focused on female empowerment showed positive changes in the main indicators including female decision-making power and physical abuse. The majority of these studies that examined the impact on employment showed significant increases in working-age adult labour participation and significant decreases in elderly adults and children. Because impacts on poverty, employment, education and empowerment would primarily influence individual livelihoods and thus the affordability and accessibility of food, these results suggest that the impact of cash transfers on the second dimension of food security is strongly positive. The significant impacts in the majority of studies on dietary diversity, stunting (height for age) and health service use also indicate a positive influence on food utilisation, the third dimension of food security. The impacts on savings, livestock accumulation, agricultural asset accumulation, agricultural inputs, and business and enterprise were also significantly positive in the majority of studies that examined these indicators, suggesting a potentially strong and positive influence on production and productivity, and thus on the first dimension of food security, food availability.

This analysis therefore suggests that successful policy interventions for the relief of famine and hunger are those based on the needs of the individuals, households and families involved. While immediate relief of these needs will be warranted in many situations, possibly in the form of direct food aid or direct income supplements where food markets are still functioning effectively, solutions for the intermediate and longer term must seek to restore their exchange entitlements. This will require setting in place mechanisms and processes that effectively restore and reconstruct their asset base, in terms of human capital (education and training), physical and financial capital (provision of credit facilities) and, in some instances, social capital (community interventions, cooperative institutions, policies focused on social and economic inclusion). In this context, help for smallholder farmers provides an important focus for a successful intervention strategy.

References

Adato, M., Carter, M. R. and May, J. 2006. Exploring Poverty Traps and Exclusion in South Africa Using Qualitative and Quantitative Data. *Journal of Development Studies*, 42, 226–247.

Arrow, K. J., Dasgupta, P. and Maler, K. G. 2003. Evaluating Projects and Assessing Sustainable Development in Imperfect Economies. *Environmental & Resource Economics*, 26, 647–685.

Barrett, C. B. and Carter, M. R. 2013. The Economics of Poverty Traps and Persistent Poverty: Empirical and Policy Implications. *Journal of Development Studies*, 49, 976–990.

Barrett, C. B., Marenya, P. P., McPeak, J., Minten, B., Murithi, F., Olouch-Kosura, W., Place, F., Randrianarisoa, J. C., Rasambainarivo, J. and Wangila, J. 2006. Welfare Dynamics in Rural Kenya and Madagascar. *Journal of Development Studies*, 42, 248–277.

Barrientos, A. 2013. *Social Assistance in Developing Countries*. Cambridge: Cambridge University Press.

Bastagli, F., Hagen-Zanker, J., Harman, L., Barca, V., Sturge, G., Schmidt, T. and Pellerano, L. 2016. *Cash Transfers: What Does the Evidence Say? A Rigorous Review of Programme Impact and of the Role of Design and Implementation Features*. London: Overseas Development Institute.

Baulch, B. 1987. Entitlements and the Wollo Famine of 1982–1985. *Disasters*, 11, 195–204.

Bowbrick, P. 1986. The Causes of Famine: A Refutation of Professor Sen's Theory. *Food Policy*, 11, 105–124.

Bowles, S., Durlaf, S. and Hoff, K. (eds.) 2006. *Poverty Traps*. New York: Russell Sage Foundation.

Corbett, J. 1988. Famine and Household Coping Strategies. *World Development*, 16, 1099–1112.

Cutler, P. 1984. Famine Forecasting: Prices and Peasant Behaviour in Northern Ethiopia. *Disasters*, 8, 48–56.

Dasgupta, P. and Ray, D. 1986. Inequality as a Determinant of Malnutrition and Unemployment: Theory. *Economic Journal*, 96, 1011–1034.

Devereux, S. 1988. Entitlements, Availability and Famine: A Revisionist View of Wollo, 1972–74. *Food Policy*, 13, 270–282.

Devereux, S. 2001. Sen's Entitlement Approach: Critiques and Counter-Critiques. *Oxford Development Studies*, 29, 245–263.

Fan, S., Pandya-Lorch, R. and Yosef, S. (eds.) 2014. *Resilience for Food and Nutrition Security*. Washington, DC: International Food Policy Research Institute.

FAO. 2015. *The State of Agricultural Commodity Markets: Trade and Food Security: Achieving a Better Balance Between National Priorities and the Collective Good*. Rome: FAO.

Gillson, I. and Fouad, A. (eds.) 2015. *Trade Policy and Food Security: Improving Access to Food in Developing Countries in the Wake of High World Prices*. Washington, DC: World Bank.

Hanlon, J., Barrientos, A. and Hulme, D. 2010. *Just Give Money to the Poor: The Development Revolution From the Global South*. Sterling, VA: Kumarian Press.

Hickey, S. and Du Toit, A. 2013. Adverse Incorporation, Social Exclusion and Chronic Poverty. *In:* Shepherd, A. and Brunt, J. (eds.) *Chronic Poverty: Concepts, Causes and Policy*. New York: Palgrave Macmillan.

Kim, D-H. 2011. Trade, Growth and Income. *The Journal of International Trade and Economic Development*, 20, 677–709.

Kraay, A. and McKenzie, D. 2014. Do Poverty Traps Exist? Assessing the Evidence. *Journal of Economic Perspectives*, 28, 127–148.

Kula, E. 1988. The Inadequacy of the Entitlement Approach to Explain and Remedy Famines. *Journal of Development Studies*, 25, 112–117.

McCorriston, S., Hemming, D. J., Lamontagne-Godwin, J. D., Osborn, J., Parr, M. J. and Roberts, P. D. 2013. *What Is the Evidence of the Impact of Trade Liberalisation on Food Security in Developing Countries? A Systematic Review*. London: EPPI-Centre, Social Science Research Unit, Institute of Education, University of London.

Mousseau, F. and Mittal, A. 2006. *Sahel: A Prisoner of Starvation? A Case Study of the 2005 Food Crisis in Niger*. Oakland, CA: Oakland Institute.

Nolan, P. 1993. The Causation and Prevention of Famines: A Critique of A. K. Sen. *Journal of Peasant Studies*, 21, 21–28.

Osmani, S. R. 1993. The Entitlement Approach to Famine: An Assessment. *Working Papers No 107*. Helsinki: United Nations University, World Institute for Development Economics Research.

Rubin, O. 2009. The Niger Famine: A Collapse of Entitlements and Democratic Responsiveness. *Journal of Asian and African Studies*, 44, 279–298.

Rubin, O. 2016. *Contemporary Famine Analysis*. New York: Springer.

Sen, A. 1980. Famines. *World Development*, 8, 613–621.

Sen, A. 1981a. Ingredients of Famine Analysis – Availability and Entitlements. *Quarterly Journal of Economics*, 96, 433–464.

Sen, A. 1981b. *Poverty and Famines: An Essay on Entitlement and Deprivation*. Oxford: Clarendon Press.

Sen, A. 1982. Famines. *Development-Seeds of Change-Village Through Global Order*, 4, 34–36.

Sen, A. 1987. *Hunger and Entitlements*. Helsinki, Finland: World Institute for Development Economics Research of the United Nations University.

Sen, A. 2002. Why Half the Planet Is Hungry. *Observer of London*. London.

United Nations. 2015. *The Millenium Development Goals Report 2015*. New York: United Nations.

Von Braun, J., Vargas Hill, R. and Pandya-Lorch, R. (eds.) 2009. *The Poorest and the Hungry: Assessments, Analyses, and Actions*. Washington, DC: International Food Policy Research Institute.

Watts, M. 1983. *Silent Violence: Food, Famine and Peasantry in Northern Nigeria*. Berkeley: University of California Press.

You, J. 2017. Asset-Based Poverty Transition and Persistence in Rural China. *Agricultural Economics*, 48, 219–239.

5 Food utilisation and nutrition security

Introduction

As pointed out by Barrett (2010) the third pillar of food security, food utilisation, is concerned with the extent to which individuals and households are able to make good use of the food that they can command. This means that households are consuming foods that are nutritionally essential and these foods have been prepared safely and appropriately under sanitary conditions to deliver their full nutritional value. It also means that those consuming the food are sufficiently healthy that they can absorb and metabolise the nutrients that they need.

Just as food availability does not guarantee food on the table for households, the affordability of food for all does not guarantee adequate nutrition. Individuals and households must also have the relevant knowledge and skills and sufficient equipment and infrastructure to use properly the food they have acquired. This evolution in thinking, from 'food security' to 'food and nutrition security', is illustrated in recent publications from policy making institutions, such as IFPRI (International Food Policy Research Institute, 2016) and the World Bank (World Bank, 2013), and a report from the High Level Panel of Experts at the Committee on World Food Security (HLPE, 2016).

This increasing focus on "Food and Nutrition Security" marks a switch in emphasis from the traditional concentration on the first two pillars, food availability (the "Food First" approach) and food affordability (the "Livelihoods First" approach), to the third pillar, food utilisation. There is also a move towards recasting and extending the remit of this pillar to consider another step in the food consumption chain, how food contributes to human activity and functioning.

A variety of issues is subsumed under this topic. These include the way diets have changed as countries become more affluent (the nutrition transition) and how this is leading to increased prevalence of obesity and an increase in noncommunicable 'lifestyle' diseases, such as diabetes and heart disease (the epidemiological transition) (Popkin and Gordon-Larsen, 2004). Also included are the roles of information and household infrastructure in promoting good nutrition and the role of nutrition in supporting individual productivity and the livelihoods on which families and households depend. The persistence of micronutrient deficiencies and the high level of losses and waste of edible food in the food value chain are also considered here.

The FAO et al. (2013) recognise that there are two distinct facets to food utilisation. An "inputs" approach reflects a focus on indicators of food quality and the preparation, health and hygiene conditions that determine effective food utilisation and the prevalence of food losses and waste. By contrast, an "outcomes" focus is captured by anthropometric indicators of under-nutrition (mainly available for children under five years), measuring one or more of stunting (being short for one's age), wasting (being thin for one's height) and underweight (being thin for one's age) and of over-nutrition and obesity.

This chapter therefore sets out to discuss issues related to micronutrient deficiency and hidden hunger in the next section, followed by consideration of the relationships between food, nutrition and individual productivity in the third section of this chapter. The fourth section then considers the increase in obesity and the extent of non-communicable lifestyle diseases in both developing and developed economies. The management of food waste and the need to conserve nutrients is discussed in the fifth section, and the final section summarises this chapter and considers a number of key implications for policy interventions.

Micronutrient deficiency and hidden hunger

The focus up to this point has been on the availability of energy and protein (generally referred to as 'macronutrients'), since these are consumed in significant quantities and are major contributors to human nutrition and wellbeing. In fact, measures of hunger and under-nutrition have concentrated on energy availability, recognising that in practice, the overwhelming majority of diets that meet people's energy requirements will also meet protein requirements. However, as pointed out by Biesalski (2013), there is increasing evidence of nutrition problems arising from insufficient consumption of a wide range of other nutrients that are consumed in much smaller quantities but nevertheless make unique and irreplaceable contributions to human development and wellbeing, especially among growing children and pregnant and lactating mothers. In fact, estimates suggest that this type of micronutrient deficiency affects between two billion and three billion people globally (Biesalski, 2013; Stein and Qaim, 2007; Von Grebmer et al., 2014). Yet, despite its widespread prevalence, members of the public do not generally recognise it as a problem. More importantly, policy makers and political decision makers, often in spite of unambiguous evidence of its existence and impacts, do not always acknowledge it as a problem worthy of attention. This goes some way to explaining why the problem continues to be referred to as hidden. Further explanation might be based on the condition being difficult to recognise and its main impacts being subject to significant delays and, in many cases, being easily attributable to other causes.

The exact nature of these problems varies widely from person to person, time to time, and place to place, depending on which micronutrients are lacking in the diet. According to Biesalski, the human body extracts 51 essential compounds from food. These include a range of amino acids and 19 other micronutrients, such as vitamins, trace elements and minerals. Research has shown that these compounds exert a direct influence on the physical and mental development of humans, including development of the immune system and of essential metabolic processes. However, the precise causal pathways are largely unknown and still subject to research and investigation. In fact, only a few conditions have been shown to be unambiguously caused by micronutrient deficiencies, for example, scurvy (vitamin C deficiency), rickets (lack of vitamin D), beriberi (insufficient vitamin B in the diet) and pellagra (niacin deficiency). Other recognisable symptoms of hidden hunger mainly arise through insufficient dietary content of vitamin A (blindness in children and night blindness in adults), iodine (goitre and thyroid problems) and iron (anaemia and related conditions). Zinc is also an important factor contributing to a number of conditions, but in this case, the causal chain is much more complex, so establishing direct causality is difficult.

The focus of analysis and policy intervention for dealing with hidden hunger has been shifting over recent decades. This has mainly come as a move away from a static framework constructed around concepts of food security and nutritional deficiency with a focus on the provision of sufficient energy and specific nutrients. A more dynamic framework considers how the problem evolves over time for specific households and individuals and focuses on their vulnerability and the intergenerational consequences of hunger and undernourishment. An important milestone in this shift was the publication in 2008 of a special five-part series on nutrition by the *Lancet* (Horton, 2008). This series of papers started from the point of view that nutrition had become a desperately neglected aspect of the care for maternal, new-born and child health and set out to fill a perceived gap in global health and policy action. The authors of these papers pointed in particular to a "golden interval for intervention" during the first 1,000 days of life, from pregnancy to two years of age, and proposed that a major international effort be undertaken to implement a number of well-known and well-proven nutritional interventions to reduce stunting and micronutrient deficiencies. In addition, they proposed that governments and other institutions and agencies set up systems and institutions to scale up these interventions to national levels. They also considered that complementary interventions for the empowerment of women and for the enhancement of trade, agriculture and poverty reduction were essential to the success of the policies to eliminate undernutrition. Following directly from these proposals, a broad collaborative effort by the World Bank, United Nations Children's Fund (UNICEF), World Health Organization (WHO), World Food Programme (WFP), and a number of governments, organisations and agencies has developed a framework that incorporates principles, priorities and key considerations to guide nutritional interventions at the country level (Annonymous, 2010). By 2010, 28 countries were collaborating to improve the effectiveness of their inter-disciplinary nutrition interventions as part of the Scaling Up Nutrition (SUN) movement (SUN Movement Secretariat, 2012), and this number had expanded to 58 in January 2017.

Food, nutrition and productivity

As we suggested above the problem of hunger alleviation and prevention is ultimately a problem of ensuring that all people everywhere are able to obtain the nutrients they need for a healthy and active life. While having sufficient food available is necessary to achieve this, it is also necessary that people can afford to purchase the food that they need and they are not prevented from consuming it by social customs or by political or legal discrimination. Furthermore, it is now recognised that getting food to the household does not ensure adequate nutrition for all the household's members. Potential problems arise for a range of different reasons.

The availability of equipment and knowledge (physical and human capital) at household level is important here. For example, inadequate processing and cooking procedures can lead to nutrients being depleted or becoming unavailable. This may be attributable to deficiencies in food preparation and storage facilities and related infrastructure. At the same time, lack of knowledge and experience in the management of household nutrition, especially for young children and other vulnerable groups, may also be a factor. The health of individuals and the infrastructure that supports healthy individuals is an essential part of the necessary human and physical capital. The availability of clean water and sanitation as well as satisfactory and accessible health care facilities is also important here.

The outcome of intra-household food allocation decisions can also contribute to problems (Agarwal and Herring, 2013). In circumstances of food scarcity, sharing the limited available food among members of the household will likely be biased in favour of those seen to contribute most to household livelihoods and wellbeing. This rational household survival strategy means that those seen as making a less essential contribution to the perceived immediate needs of the household will be allocated smaller shares of the available food. As food scarcity intensifies, these groups may become severely undernourished. These decisions will have major implications for the nutrition status of vulnerable groups, such as female members of the household, children and the elderly. The implications for the nutritional status of pregnant and lactating mothers and for young children have particularly significant implications for the productivity and cognitive development of the next generation of adults and consequent knock-on effects on food and nutrition security. This raises the possibility of a nutrition-related inter-generational trap (a type of 'hunger trap') paralleling the livelihood traps described in the previous chapter (Dasgupta, 2009) – but see Kraay and McKenzie (2014) and the earlier discussion of these issues in Chapter 4.

These issues have also been highlighted by Dasgupta and Ray (1987) and by Dasgupta (1993), who goes on to consider the crucial role of nutrition in supporting the productivity and livelihoods of individuals, households and families. To begin with, he emphasises the complementarity between individual macronutrients and individual micronutrients, pointing out that a significant number of micronutrients are essential and that adequate nutrition requires both protein and energy in sufficient quantities. He also points out further complementarity between the provision of nutrients, the availability of knowledge and infrastructure, as discussed above, and the availability of sanitation and health care. This supports freedom from infectious diseases, especially those diseases that can undermine even the adequate provision of both micronutrients and macronutrients, such as gastro-enteritis and diarrhoea. The importance of ensuring adequate nutrition for infants and for pregnant and lactating mothers is also emphasised here, and it is made clear that this remains a problem in developed countries as well as in developing countries (Biesalski and Black, 2016).

Obesity and the epidemiological transition

The nutrition transition, its influence on dietary patterns and implications for food demand and food security, has been highlighted in earlier chapters. There we emphasised the shift away from traditional diets based on carbohydrate rich staples towards an increase in the consumption of meat and animal products, vegetable oils and fresh vegetables and fruit. Another aspect of this transition, also highlighted in Popkin (1993), is the convergence of diets in developed and developing countries to a diet high in saturated fat, sugar and refined foods with a low fibre content. This has been associated with a shift in societal patterns of disease, with declining prevalence of infectious diseases associated with malnutrition and poor sanitation and an increase in the prevalence of chronic and degenerative diseases associated with modern lifestyles, often referred to as the 'epidemiological transition' (Omran, 1971).

While this transition and accompanying problems of obesity and the increased prevalence of lifestyle diseases were initially seen as a problem mainly for the high-income developed countries, it has become clear in recent years that these changes are now occurring in developing countries. In fact, as pointed out by Popkin and Gordon-Larsen (2004), these changes are occurring at greater speed and at earlier stages in the economic and social development of these countries than had been the case for the earlier transition in the developed countries. More importantly, there is now evidence that obesity is becoming a problem for younger people as well as for adults and older people.

The case for government intervention in these circumstances has been investigated by Griffith and O'Connell (2010) who point out that while most people agree that individuals are in the best position to maximise their wellbeing by their choice of foods to eat, a case for public policy intervention can be made when there are market failures. In the case of food markets, they point to two potential failures. In the first place, information and cognitive failures arise when people are not well informed about the nutrient characteristics of individual food products, about their own nutritional needs or about the potential costs of consuming particular foods, especially when these costs are uncertain and accrue in the future. Secondly, externalities arise where the individual does not bear the full costs of making poor decisions about their own food consumption. In particular, individuals may not bear the full costs of any health problems that arise because of their consumption decisions, and any reduction in productivity represents an economic loss for the rest of society.

They discuss three potential policy interventions. Firstly, education and other efforts to counteract information and cognitive failures can include general advertising campaigns providing unbiased dietary and shopping advice, as well as more targeted campaigns. These may be aimed at educating mothers with young children, or older adults or schoolchildren and teenagers etc. Secondly, policies aimed at changing relative prices to make unhealthy foods less desirable to consumers can include taxes based on harmful ingredients (such as saturated fats) to reduce the possible weight gain associated with consuming particular foods or a tax on specific products, such as carbonated drinks or potato crisps. In principle, the idea here is to ensure that the private cost to the individual of consuming these products matches more closely the full costs to society of this consumption. Thirdly, regulation of firms involved in the production, processing, advertising and selling of these products. However, they point to implementation difficulties in imperfectly competitive food markets, arising from the market power of food processors and retailers and their use of this power to counteract the impact of the policies through pricing and promotion activities.

More importantly, as pointed out by Smith and Tasnadi (2014), the influence of food industry groups on the obesity debate can be quite pervasive. Their profit maximising lobbying efforts extend beyond traditional attempts to influence regulators to include activities designed to modify public perceptions of the industry, including media coverage, industry-related research and advertising campaigns. They suggest that this phenomenon can be labelled 'deep capture', since it goes beyond the traditional notion of regulatory capture where industry representatives seek to influence government regulators to provide favourable treatment for the industry.

Mazzocchi et al. (2009) and Traill (2012), while broadly in agreement with this analysis, emphasise that information and education programmes, on their own, can change knowledge and attitudes, but there is limited evidence about their ability to change individual behaviour. These interventions may nevertheless lead to an increase in consumer welfare by enabling better informed, if still unhealthy, food choices. The need for a basic background regulatory system that focuses on nutrition labelling and advertising controls is also emphasised. However, they suggest that market interventions provide a more direct and more effective means of tackling obesity and the externalities imposed on society by unhealthy eating. They further emphasise that reducing obesity is more likely with a combination of policies. Taxes on high-energy foods will lead to reduction in the consumption of these foods. At the same time, a subsidy on the consumption of healthy food (for example, fruit and vegetables) will further encourage a switch from unhealthy to healthy eating. However, this combination of 'fat taxes' and 'thin subsidies' has a doubly regressive impact, since those with lower incomes tend to consume both more unhealthy food and less healthy food than those with higher incomes.

Sassi (2010), reporting on a study of obesity trends and interventions across OECD countries, also focuses on multi-intervention strategies and stresses the cost-effectiveness of intervention packages that simultaneously target a range of age groups and multiple determinants of obesity. He also finds that fiscal measures provide consistently larger gains in health and longevity for those on lower incomes, though the impact of other interventions varies between countries.

Discussion of obesity and overconsumption of energy-saturated diets sits uneasily with most other topics and the overall theme of this book: hunger, underconsumption of food and energy-deficient diets. Yet this topic cannot be ignored or brushed aside, since it represents an emerging problem of malnutrition for which no clear solution has yet been devised. Moreover, although it is often regarded as a developed-country problem, there is ample evidence that it is becoming ever more important in developing countries (Popkin and Gordon-Larsen, 2004) and may well impose costs on their economies that equal or exceed those currently being imposed by hunger and under-nutrition.

Food loss, waste and the conservation of nutrients

The problem of food waste and its implications for food security are only recently being highlighted and are beginning to emerge as a potential concern for national and international policy makers. At this stage, however, there is only limited information on the extent of this problem across the globe, though current rough estimates suggest that it could account for as much as one third of total food production (HLPE, 2014; Gustavsson et al., 2011). This is extremely significant in current circumstances: for example, dealing effectively with this problem could reduce, by 25 per cent or more, the need to expand production to meet projected food needs in 2050.

It is generally agreed that food waste is that proportion of edible food products intended for human consumption and passing through the food value chain, which has been discarded, degraded, lost or consumed by pests. The inedible or undesirable components in foodstuffs are not included here. Some would argue for a distinction between food loss, which occurs in the early parts of the food value chain, and food waste, occurring in the later stages closer to consumption. In this perspective, food loss would refer to 'leakage' and degradation in the production, storage, transport and processing stages; food waste would involve leakage and degradation at the higher end of the value chain, in retail and final consumption (Bond et al., 2013).

Food loss and waste per person are much higher in industrialised countries than in developing countries. In Europe and North America, waste by consumers is estimated to amount to about 95–115 kilogrammes per person per year, whereas the corresponding figure for Sub-Saharan Africa and South/Southeast Asia is no more than 6–11 kilogrammes per person per year. Furthermore, most food loss and waste in developing countries can be attributed to financial, managerial and technical limitations in harvesting, storage, and cooling facilities, and to infrastructural deficiencies in the packaging and marketing systems. This indicates a need for strengthening the supply and value chains and the increase in investment in transportation infrastructure and in processing and packaging facilities. Gustavsson et al. (2011) suggest that both public and private sectors need to participate in these investment activities.

In the developed, industrialised countries, food losses and wastes are mainly attributable to the behaviour of consumers and to a lack of coordination between actors along the supply and value chain. This includes the contribution of farmer-buyer sales agreements, where quality standards based on cosmetics rather than substantive elements of food quality can lead to rejection of large quantities of edible food. Lack of planning by consumers to consume purchases before expiry of 'use by' dates and a generally careless attitude to food also contribute to significant amounts of waste.

The causes of food loss and waste can be classified more broadly in a number of different ways. However, it is important to distinguish between the cause of a particular type of loss or waste and the stage in the food value chain at which the loss or waste is observed. It is quite possible that any particular observed loss, at a particular stage in the value chain, could have been caused by activities that took place in a previous stage in the chain. For example, waste at the retail or consumption stages may be directly attributable to processes used (or misused) at the harvest stage. In addition, waste can result from a wide range of other processes at other stages in the chain, including those related to biological, chemical, mechanical, technological, organisational or behavioural processes. This emphasises the need to take a very broad view of the entire food system when considering how to reduce or prevent food loss and waste. HLPE (2014) point to a situation where lack of care in handling fruit at harvest and packaging, possibly related to poor working conditions for harvesters and packers, can reduce shelf life and increase the amount of fruit that needs to be disposed of by the retailer or consumer. Alternatively, a retailer's decision to lower its buying price, increase quality standards or otherwise interrupt a contract may mean vegetables left to rot in the fields and subsequently ploughed in. These are rather simplistic examples of what can occur in the complex relationships between various members of the food value chain.

In trying to disentangle this complexity, HLPE (2014) classify the causes of food waste into three categories:

'Micro-level' causes lead to waste at each specific stage in the chain (from production through to consumption), that arises because of actions or inaction of individuals and other actors at the same stage in the chain. This may or may not be in response to external influences.

'Meso-level' causes are secondary causes or structural causes that arise at another stage in the chain other than the stage at which the waste is observed, and can generate Micro-level causes.

'Macro-level' causes account for food waste arising from more systematic issues and problems, including malfunctioning of the food system in general, and lack of incentives or coordination among actors in the value chain to facilitate investments or the adoption of good practice. This level of causes contributes to the emergence of problems at Meso-level or Micro-level.

HLPE (2014) suggest the main approach to solving these problems requires better integration of the food system and its value chain. In particular, they suggest actions along four parallel and mutually supporting tracks, undertaken with the full cooperation of all the actors in the chain. These include:

1) improvement of data collection on food waste and the sharing of information among all members of the value chain;
2) construction of strategies to reduce waste at specific levels in the chain;
3) institution of specific activities to reduce waste where feasible, including infrastructure investments and the development of regulatory frameworks to

protect the interests of the smaller and more vulnerable participants in the food value chain;

4) improving the coordination of policies and strategies to reduce food loss and waste.

Developing specific approaches to solving these problems will require a significant amount of additional information about the extent and distribution of food loss and waste across the food system and across countries and regions. A better understanding is also required of the complexities of the food value chain and interactions between strategies for changing the behaviour of producers, processors, marketers and consumers.

Summary and policy implications

The changing emphasis in the analysis of food security problems and policies from a food-focused approach (Chapter 3), to a livelihoods-focused approach (Chapter 4) to a nutrition-focused approach (this chapter) marks the evolution in motivation and thinking among the global food policy community and the researchers that support them. This chapter has taken on board the more recent concerns among the policy community for the third pillar of food security by focusing on the 'utilisation' of food available and affordable in providing adequate nutrition to households and individuals.

We point out that a variety of issues are subsumed under this topic including issues related to micronutrient deficiency and hidden hunger. The Scaling Up Nutrition (SUN) movement is an important international initiative addressing these issues within a collaborative international and inter-disciplinary framework. Other important issues are those arising from the relationship between food, nutrition and productivity. These indicate the need to ensure that households and individuals have command over sufficient knowledge and infrastructure to transform available and affordable food into adequate and balanced nutrient streams. In this way, they can ensure healthy growth and development of younger members of the family and ensure sufficient productivity among the adults to support the livelihoods needed to sustain these nutrient streams. We also discuss issues arising from the nutrition transition discussed earlier in Chapter 2, focusing at this stage on the obesity problems and the epidemiological transition that has accompanied these changes. We discuss the case for government intervention in food markets to counter the harmful effects of these changes including the use of specific policy instruments based on education and information, taxes and subsidies, and regulation. We note that, given a basic system of advertising controls and nutrition labelling, taxes and subsidies are generally more effective at changing people's food consumption behaviour. However, the effects of food industry lobbying on regulation and on public perceptions of the industry may dampen the impact of these policies. Finally, we consider food loss and waste and, with the limited information available, discuss its distribution across the globe, possible causes and approaches that may help extend our knowledge of these problems and of the interventions that may be used to effectively counter them.

References

Agarwal, B. and Herring, R. 2013. Food Security, Productivity and Gender Inequality. *In:* Herring, R. J. (ed.) *The Oxford Handbook of Food, Politics and Society.* New York: Oxford University Press.

Anonymous. 2010. Scaling Up Nutrition: A Framework for Action. *Food and Nutrition Bulletin*, 31, 178–186.

Barrett, C. B. 2010. Measuring Food Insecurity. *Science*, 327, 825–828.

Biesalski, H. K. 2013. *Hidden Hunger.* Berlin: Springer-Verlag.

Biesalski, H. K. and Black, R. E. (eds.) 2016. *Hidden Hunger: Malnutrition and the First 1,000 Days of Life: Causes, Consequences, and Solutions.* Basel: New York: Karger.

Bond, M., Meacham, T., Bhunnoo, R. and Benton, T. G. 2013. Food Waste Within Global Food Systems. *Global Food Security Programme.*

Dasgupta, P. 1993. *An Inquiry into Well-Being and Destitution.* Oxford: Oxford University Press.

Dasgupta, P. 2009. Poverty Traps: Exploring the Complexity of Causation. *In:* Von Braun, J., Hill, R. V. and Pandya-Lorch, R. (eds.) *The Poorest and the Hungry: Assessments, Analyses, and Actions.* Washington, DC: IFPRI.

Dasgupta, P. and Ray, D. 1987. Inequality as a Determinant of Malnutrition and Unemployment: Policy. *Economic Journal*, 97, 177–188.

FAO, IFAD and WFP. 2013. *The State of Food Insecurity in the World 2013: The Multiple Dimensions of Food Insecurity.* Rome: FAO.

Griffith, R. and O'Connell, M. 2010. Public Policy Towards Food Consumption. *Fiscal Studies*, 31, 481–507.

Gustavsson, J., Cederberg, C., Stonesson, U., Van Otterdijk, R. and Meybeck, A. 2011. *Global Food Losses and Food Waste – Extent, Causes and Prevention.* Rome: FAO.

HLPE. 2014. Food Losses and Waste in the Context of Sustainable Food Systems. *Report of the High Level Panel of Experts on Food Security and Nutrition of the Committee on World Food Security.* Rome.

HLPE. 2016. Sustainable Agricultural Development for Food Security and Nutrition: What Roles for Livestock? *Report by the High Level Panel of Experts on Food Security and Nutrition of the Committee on World Food Security.* Rome.

Horton, R. 2008. Maternal and Child Undernutrition: An Urgent Opportunity. *Lancet*, 371, 179.

International Food Policy Research Institute. 2016. *Global Nutrition Report 2016: From Promise to Impact: Ending Malnutrition by 2030.* Washington, DC: IFPRI.

Kraay, A. and McKenzie, D. 2014. Do Poverty Traps Exist? Assessing the Evidence. *Journal of Economic Perspectives*, 28, 127–148.

Mazzocchi, M., Traill, W. B. and Shogren, J. F. 2009. *Fat Economics: Nutrition Health and Economic Policy.* Oxford: Oxford University Press.

Omran, A. R. 1971. The Epidemiological Transition: A Theory of the Epidemiology of Population Change. *Millbank Memorial Fund Quarterly*, 49, 509–538.

Popkin, B. M. 1993. Nutritional Patterns and Transitions. *Population and Development Review*, 19, 138–157.

Popkin, B. M. and Gordon-Larsen, P. 2004. The Nutrition Transition: Worldwide Obesity Dynamics and Their Determinants. *International Journal of Obesity*, 28, S2–S9.

Sassi, F. 2010. *Obesity and the Economics of Prevention.* Paris: OECD.

Smith, T. G. and Tasnadi, A. 2014. The Economics of Information, Deep Capture, and the Obesity Debate. *American Journal of Agricultural Economics*, 96, 533–541.

Stein, A. J. and Qaim, M. 2007. The Human and Economic Cost of Hidden Hunger. *Food and Nutrition Bulletin*, 28, 125–134.

SUN Movement Secretariat. 2012. *SUN Movement Progress Report 2011–2012*. Geneva: SUN Movement Secretariat.

Traill, W. B. 2012. Economic Perspectives on Nutrition Policy Evaluation. *Journal of Agricultural Economics*, 63, 505–527.

Von Grebmer, K., Saltzman, A., Birol, E., Wiesmann, D. M., Prasai, N., Yin, S., Yohannes, Y., Menon, P., Thompson, J. and Sonntag, A. 2014. *2014 Global Hunger Index: The Challenge of Hidden Hunger*. Bonn, Washington, DC and Dublin: Welthungerhilfe, International Food Policy Research Institute, and Concern Worldwide.

World Bank. 2013. *Scaling Up Nutrition: A Framework for Action*. Washington, DC: World Bank.

6 Stability, sustainability and resilience

Introduction

Previous chapters of this book have traced the evolution in thinking about food security from an exclusive focus on food production and the availability of food at the national and global levels (Chapter 3) through concerns about affordability of food and the livelihoods of people (Chapter 4). More recently, the emphasis of research and the concerns of policy makers relate to issues of food utilisation and the ability of individuals and households to use the food that is available and affordable to provide the nutrients needed for healthy growth and development and an active and productive life (Chapter 5).

What this means is that the focus of policy makers has shifted from 'food security' to 'food and nutrition security'. However, even if food is available, affordable and efficiently utilised, continuing welfare of individuals is assured only if these components are stable and sustainable. For this reason, our obligation to feed those who are hungry must include a commitment to ensure that processes supporting food security remain stable over time. In addition, to ensure stability over time, it is essential these processes are sustainable and resilient to shocks and stresses arising from the broader social, economic, biological and physical systems in which they are embedded. Consequently, our discussions in this chapter consider as constituent parts of the fourth dimension of food and nutrition security, the stability, sustainability and resilience, of food availability, affordability and utilisation.

This dimension focuses on the extent to which the availability, affordability and proper utilisation of food continues over time. A key distinction here is that, for individuals and families, food security failure and hunger can be transitory, seasonal or chronic, and this may be the result of problems with any one of the other three dimensions separately or in combination.

For example, transitory hunger can arise when food becomes unavailable due to problems at the food production level; when natural disasters and drought result in crop failure and decreased food availability; when civil conflicts decrease access to food; or when instability in markets result in food-price spikes that generate transitory problems with food affordability. Another factor that can lead to temporary hunger is loss of employment or productivity, caused by illness or by temporary economic problems. In addition, without an efficient trading and storage system, seasonal hunger can also result from the regular pattern of growing seasons in food production, when all food from the previous harvest has been consumed before food from the next harvest becomes available. On the other hand, chronic (or permanent) food insecurity and hunger are characterised by the long-term persistent lack of adequate food, where individuals and households are constantly at risk of being unable to acquire food to meet the needs of all. Chronic and transitory food insecurity are linked, since the recurrence of transitory food insecurity can make households more vulnerable to chronic hunger.

In this chapter, we want to consider alternative notions of stability and sustainability and the implications of explicitly including these notions in the design and operation of policies to alleviate food insecurity. In particular, this chapter is about delineating how current approaches to food security policy may need to adjust if fully stable and sustainable solutions are to be engendered and supported.

In the next section we consider the variability over recent decades of food availability in relation to food requirements, reflected mainly in the volatility of food prices. The third section then considers an intuitive notion of sustainability, centred on the idea of continuity over time. From an economics perspective this entails conserving the aggregate stock of productive assets. However, when we need to conserve a specific portfolio of assets rather the overall stock, we switch to considering an ecological approach and the need for resilience in ecological and socioeconomic systems. In the fourth section, we explore the measurement of sustainability and resilience in agricultural and food systems and consider how the global food system can provide sustaiable and resilient solutions to the problem of feeding the hungry. The final section summarises the discussion and explores implications for policy intervention.

Stability and price volatility

Traditionally, the fourth dimension of food security has involved consideration of the stability of food production and prices. The spikes in food prices towards the end of the last decade have drawn particular attention to this aspect of food security.

Food prices across the world began to rise in late summer 2006, increasing dramatically from January 2007 (Figure 6.1) and nearly doubling by June 2008. This rise in food prices was seen as a significant factor triggering riots in a variety of places across the globe, including Egypt, Haiti and Cameroon, as well as extensive protests, some violent, on Ivory Coast and in Mozambique, Mauritania, Senegal, Uzbekistan, Bolivia and Indonesia (Adam, 2008). Prices rose again from May 2010, peaking in February 2011 at similar levels to June 2008 and again in August 2012, peaking at even higher levels, yet this time not accompanied by civil unrest. However, there has been a broad tendency for civil unrest to be associated with food price increases (though not with increased food price volatility) over the two decades 1990 to 2011 (Bellemare, 2014).

A number of authors have discussed the underlying causes of these increases. Among a long list of possible causal factors, they pay special attention to the diversion of food crops as feedstocks for biofuel (Abbot et al., 2008; Wright, 2014b). They also consider the impact of rapid economic growth, particularly in China,

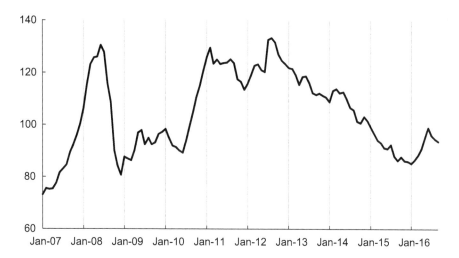

Figure 6.1 Nominal monthly world food prices index: January 2007 – August 2016, (2010 = 100)

Source: World Bank

that has generated increased demand for agricultural commodities and a low ratio of grain inventories to grain consumption, and to the impact of trade restrictions (Piesse and Thirtle, 2009). In addition, they consider the influence of speculation in commodity markets more generally (Gilbert, 2010; Cooke and Nobles, 2009), underinvestment in agriculture and poor harvests in Australia (Wright, 2014a).

However, the principal interest in this chapter is less on the reasons for rapid increase in prices and more on an assessment of price trends over the longer run and an assessment of possible changes in the volatility of prices. Figure 6.2 presents real annual world food prices over the period 1960 to 2016, based on constant 2005 US dollar prices of a wide range of food commodities. This shows a general downward movement of prices over this period and little evidence of increased volatility, even with a tendency for prices to increase since around 2000 and the recent series of price spikes as discussed in the previous paragraph. These data have been analysed in some detail by Gilbert and Morgan (2010), who show that price variability over the most recent two decades, excluding the special case of rice prices, has been consistent with experience over the longer historical period. In fact, they find that volatility has declined in recent years when compared with the situation in the 1970s and 1980s. More generally, they note that even with the substantial variability in the prices of many products over 2007–2009, of the 19 product categories that were subject to detailed statistical and econometric analysis, conditional price variances increased significantly only for three of these: groundnut oil, soya beans and soya bean oil.

A detailed analysis of food price increases and volatility has also been undertaken by Tadasse et al. (2016). Their analysis shows that exogenous shocks to supply and demand, as well as the linkages between food, energy and financial

Figure 6.2 Real annual world food prices index: 1960–2016 (2005 US dollars; 2010 = 100)
Source: World Bank

markets, have a part to play in explaining changes in price volatility and the emergence of food price spikes. However, their analysis also shows that, while speculative activity has had a significant and positive influence on price spikes, it has had no significant influence on price volatility.

A detailed review of policies to address price volatility in the context of food security has been provided by FAO et al. (2011). However, this research emphasises that some volatility in agricultural prices is essential if the production and marketing system is to cope efficiently and adequately with the mismatch between seasonal production and relatively constant demand for food and agricultural products. This is to provide incentives for storage between successive harvests and to allow prices to increase as a signal that producers should increase production when demand increases. Nevertheless, there are a variety of interventions that seek either to reduce price volatility or alternatively to mitigate its impact by helping producers and consumers to cope with it. Effective and efficient interventions are generally those that are designed to be cost effective, that allow and encourage participation by the private sector in trade and marketing of agricultural products, that are based on transparent and predictable government activities and that are carefully developed to take account of the specific circumstances in each country.

FAO et al. (2011) consider a wide range of interventions, including market information and trade policies and the establishment of buffer stocks, designed to deal with price surges emerging from shocks to domestic production. The aim is to provide timely information to public and private bodies about any emerging changes in availability and prices in domestic food markets and to facilitate the use of imports to cushion any shortfall in domestic production while providing flexible storage that will make it easier to cope with any lags in the availability of imports to domestic consumers. They also consider alternative policies that focus on helping producers to cope with likely future price volatility through effective risk management. These include the provision of agriculture research that aims to make available lower-risk technologies to producers, for example, providing stress-tolerant and disease-resistant varieties of important food crops, and increasing investment in infrastructure that reduces yield risk, such as the provision of irrigation facilities. A range of market-based insurance options are also considered, including weather-index-based insurance and the use of futures and options contracts by producers.

Perhaps the most insidious impact of volatility in food prices and the price of basic farm inputs such as fertilisers is the impact of price spikes on incomes of poor and vulnerable households. This can trigger sales of farm assets, the removal of children from school or consumption of smaller amounts of less nutritious food, with potential consequences for future productivity and future family well-being that last long after the price spikes have subsided. Given the serious and long-lasting consequences of these impacts, there are both economic and altruistic motives for the provision of an effective safety net to mitigate these impacts. Examples include school feeding programmes that can mitigate both the nutritional and potential educational impacts, mitigating the long-run effects on human capital and future economic prospects for the family.

Sustainability and resilience

The notion of sustainability has been explored in detail in the context of sustainable economic development. Much of this work is specifically focused on the sustainability of economic activities at the national level, rather than sustainability of the national and global food systems or the individual firms that make up the food value chain. We review this work here because it provides a clearly articulated notion of one key concept of sustainability. In most cases, sustainability of economic activity is considered in relation to use of natural resources and the extent to which this use can be continued into the future. This is particularly relevant for the food system, since food production is fully dependent on use of natural resources such as land, water and ecosystem services. The misuse and degradation of these resources may be part of an intensive approach to agricultural production that increases current levels of food availability and food security, but is unlikely to support these levels over an extended period and may pose a threat to the livelihoods and food security of future generations. This would indicate that current agricultural production technologies, whether modern intensive technologies or their more traditional counterparts, may not be sustainable and may not be compatible with sustainable food security.

One of the more iconic notions of sustainability is that provided by the World Commission on Environment and Development in its 1987 report (WCED, 1987). This suggests that "Sustainable development is development that meets the needs of the present without compromising the ability of future generations to meet their own needs".

Many authors have noted that, according to this definition, sustainable economic activity must involve a requirement that each generation bequeath to its successors a portfolio of productive resources that provides a range of economic opportunities no smaller than that enjoyed by itself (see, for example, Dasgupta (2010)). This can be interpreted as a state of affairs in which the wellbeing of successive generations is not declining over time (Pezzey, 1992, Arrow et al., 2004), where wellbeing is based on the flow of utility and human satisfaction from consumption. The level of consumption in turn is related to the productive capacity of the economic system, which is determined by society's current endowment of productive assets; these are made up of manufactured capital (buildings, machines, tools etc.), human capital (knowledge, skills) and natural capital (forests, groundwater, crude oil etc.) and society's institutions. Taking institutions as the structures in society that guide the allocation of resources including capital assets (Arrow et al., 2004), these will include the legal structures that govern property rights and contracts, and also the rules and norms that guide the behaviour of interpersonal networks, as well as the rules that guide the behaviour of markets and government agencies. Productive capacity will also depend on society's knowledge base including the 'library' of blueprints for constructing and organising agriculture, manufacturing, services and all commercial activity.

A clear "chain of dependence" can be identified here; human wellbeing depends on consumption, which depends on production, which depends on society's capital assets. Given that something is sustainable when we can rely on the continuity of that something into the future, a particular level of human wellbeing is sustainable if we can reliably expect that at least that level of wellbeing can be delivered over time into the future. Similarly, a particular level of overall consumption is sustainable if that level can continue to be supported into the future. This of course implies that we would require a sustainable production base, a sustainable, non-declining level of productive assets that would include human knowledge and skills, natural resources, including land, water and ecosystem services, physical capital, such as buildings and equipment, and a sustainable system of institutions.

There are two key relationships in this chain of dependence: the technological relationship between capital stocks, including natural capital stocks and consumption (via production); and the preferences of individuals which relate levels of consumption to economic welfare and human wellbeing. Changes in these relationships can be crucial in maintaining sustainability. For example, changes in productivity arising from changes in technology could lead to constant or increasing levels of consumption and human wellbeing, despite declining levels of capital stock. This means that technological change can come to the rescue of societies who deplete resources including exhaustible resources such as coal or oil etc. However, as pointed out by Pezzey (1992), sustainability can be assured in the case of continually expanding economic activity only by continual technological change to balance the increased depletion. Pezzey refers to this as a process of dynamic sustainability that depends on a 'technology treadmill'. Similarly, a continual adjustment to preferences could be sufficient to allow a constant or increasing level of human wellbeing even in the face of a declining level of consumption, a type of 'behavioural treadmill'.

This is a very brief description of the neoclassical economics approach to sustainability and this approach rests on two important assumptions. First of all, it is assumed that each category of capital asset is substitutable for every other category; a reduction in physical capital (e.g., a machine wears out or breaks down) and the consequent reduction in output can be compensated by an increase in human capital (more expertise and skill in operating the remaining machines) and so on. Where this assumption holds, it is possible to introduce a very simple sustainability criterion that requires only the preservation of the aggregate stock of capital assets across the whole economy; this is often referred to as a 'weak sustainability' criterion (Pearce and Atkinson, 1993; Victor, 1991). Even if we acknowledge that substitution is never perfect and that only a certain amount of substitution is feasible, this remains a controversial assumption. The controversy is most acute when we consider the possibility of substituting any other category of capital for natural capital; there is a wide range of circumstances when this is not feasible even to a limited extent, and many individuals would object that the contribution of natural capital assets to the economic process is unique and not substitutable. Secondly, there is an implicit assumption here that all investment and dis-investment processes are reversible. Again, most would accept that this assumption does not hold in all situations and in particular does not hold in the case of degradation of most natural assets. When neither of these assumptions is tenable, sustainability can only be assured by requiring the preservation of a specific portfolio of natural assets, a 'strong sustainability' criterion (Norton and Toman, 1997).

Norton and Toman (1997) go on to emphasise that a strong sustainability criterion is more in line with an ecological view of sustainability in contrast with the views espoused by economists for whom weak sustainability is more acceptable. They point in particular to work by a group of economists and ecologists (Arrow et al., 1995) who argue that conventional economic criteria for sustainability are not adequate for the preservation of important ecological assets. They stress in particular the importance of ecosystem resilience and its role in providing a wider range of options for future generations. The importance of resilience as a property of ecosystems is also emphasised in Common and Perrings (1992) and in Folke (2006) and explored in more detail from the perspective of sustainability in social and economic systems, by Perrings (2006) and Levin et al. (1998). These authors emphasise that resilience relates to the capacity of a system to deal with shocks, by resisting a switch between alternative equilibria, as it continues to provide basic functions. For an economic system, two such functions are generally identified (Perrings, 2006): the capacity to allocate resources efficiently as the market and supporting institutions continue to function, and the capacity to provide essential and accustomed services via the production system. The relationship between resilience and sustainability is discussed by Levin et al. (1998), who suggest that resilience has become the preferred way to consider sustainability in social as well as ecological systems in the sense that a resilient economic system is more likely to be sustainable over the longer run.

Sustainable and resilient food and nutrition security

A large number of investigators have considered the sustainability of agricultural production, across a wide range of scales and circumstances. For example, the sustainability of agricultural operations in eastern India, has been investigated at the farm level by Sharma and Sharendu (2011), the sustainability of UK arable and organic farms by Rigby et al. (2001), while progress with agricultural sustainability in a European context has been investigated by Dillon et al. (2017) and Latruffe et al. (2016). These studies consider a large number of individual indicators that measure levels of specific farm inputs, farm outputs and the characteristics of farming practices in assessing three key aspects of sustainability at the farm level. Economic sustainability considers the viability of the farm business, profitability and efficiency of resource use. Environmental sustainability considers the contribution of the farming enterprises to resource conservation and degradation and focuses especially on the impact on greenhouse gas emissions, the risk to biodiversity, and the potential role of fertiliser and chemical use in the pollution of air and water. Social sustainability is generally assessed both in terms of the contribution of farming to the viability of local communities and infrastructure and in terms of the working conditions and quality of life for farmers, farm workers and their families. In the context of food security, it is worth noting that, while these studies address the sustainability of food production, this is not the same as sustainable food availability in a particular country or region. The sustainability of any food imports needed to meet food requirements must also be considered.

A number of studies have also suggested that one important approach to ensuring adequate and sustainable food availability is to promote the intensification of agricultural production in ways that do not compromise environmental sustainability, to promote sustainable intensification. This is a response to the perceived need for additional food (as discussed in Chapter 2) and the potential difficulties in expanding the land area available for production (as discussed in Chapter 3) (Garnett, 2014; Garnett et al., 2013). A significant modification of traditional approaches to agricultural production is needed to allow increased food production while reducing the environmental impact of agricultural practices. This involves increasing yields in some areas, as well as changing management practices to encourage carbon storage, flood protection and wildlife conservation. These changes take place in the context of broader changes in the food system arising from dietary transition (see Chapter 2) and the need to consider broader nutritional issues (see Chapter 5). A range of approaches to achieving these outcomes have been discussed (Godfray and Garnett, 2014; Godfray, 2015).

The investigation of sustainability in the context of the second dimension of food security, food affordability, is not quite so straightforward. While there is a wide-ranging literature on sustainable livelihoods (Krantz, 2001; Chambers and Conway, 1992), the relationship between livelihoods and food security is a complex one, influenced by several factors, the relative importance of which can vary in different situations and over time (Woller et al., 2011). Nevertheless, there are numerous policy interventions that seek explicitly to support the sustainability and resilience of the livelihoods of vulnerable groups of people and their food security (Krantz, 2001; Office of Food for Peace, 2015; FAO, 2013). Vulnerability to poverty and the resilience of livelihoods have also been investigated (Ravallion, 1988; Morduch, 1994; Barrientos, 2013). In addition, the sustainability of food utilisation and food consumption has been investigated as part of a broader review of food system sustainability (Reisch et al., 2013; Capone et al., 2014; Vermeir and Verbeke, 2006).

Resilience is also being investigated in the context of the global agriculture and food system (Tendall et al., 2015; Bennett et al., 2014; Fan et al., 2014). Policies to improve resilience are increasingly used to confront the challenges facing the global food system, many of which have been highlighted in this and earlier chapters of this book. In its more general form, resilience refers to the ability of a system to recover quickly from shocks (Folke et al., 2002). Shocks and stresses in the food system continue to have major negative effects on those who are poor, and shocks from economic, environmental and political events appear to be becoming more frequent. Consequently, there are major efforts to establish a research and policy framework to investigate the resilience of individual households as well as the resilience of the food system and to consider what policy interventions might be most beneficial (Fan et al., 2014). This work focuses on ways in which individual producers and consumers might be helped, not just to cope better with recent and ongoing shocks, but also to become less vulnerable to the shocks expected in the future. The benefits of an efficient trading and storage system are also acknowledged, in this context, as a means of balancing needs and availability between surplus and deficit regions and time periods (Benton et al., 2017).

Recent work on the measurement of resilience, in the context of sustainable economic development, has set out to assess the ability of an economic unit to absorb shocks and resist being forced to move from a pre-existing desirable equilibrium state to one that is less desirable (Barrett and Constas, 2014; Cisse and Barrett, 2016; Barrett and Headey, 2014). An alternative approach, proposed by Smerlak and Vaitla (2017), focuses on the ability to recover from shocks and stresses, by estimating the persistence of the resulting disturbance to income or to food energy intake. Using this measure, an individual, household or region is resilient if long-term food security is not deteriorating (i.e. is sustainable according to the definition discussed in the previous section) and if the effects of shocks to food security do not persist over time. This avoids the need to provide an estimate of the presumed desirable equilibrium value but requires a significant amount of time series data to establish the food security trajectory.

Options for managing and enhancing resilience in the global system for food and nutrition security have been explored in detail by Fan et al. (2014). They consider the variety of shocks that affect food and nutrition security. These include economic shocks related to price and income volatility, environmental shocks related to weather or natural disasters, social and political shocks involving conflict, political instability and the disruption of mass migration, health shocks related to disease epidemics and many others. The available evidence suggests that these shocks are becoming more frequent and more intense, and they disproportionately affect poor and vulnerable people, threatening their livelihoods and their food and nutrition security (Zseleczky and Yosef, 2014).

There is a wide range of options available to support and enhance the ability of individuals, households, communities and societies, not only to cope with these shocks, but also to bounce back while improving their circumstances and wellbeing so that they are better prepared and less vulnerable when the next shocks arise. These options include those that focus on identifying and dealing with existing knowledge gaps and those that focus on specific policy interventions in response to specific shocks. Fan et al. (2014) consider knowledge gaps related to understanding and assessment of the mechanisms that transmit the impact of shocks and the need to monitor these shocks and to measure their impacts on those groups of people who are already poor and vulnerable. They also point to the need for a better understanding of the role of communities in the provision of social networks and the underlying social capital to support resilience. In addition, they reflect on the need for mechanisms that would help to identify better approaches to building resilience capacity.

Fan et al. (2014) also discuss potential policy interventions in response to different types of shocks. These include many of the interventions already discussed in other chapters. For example, they discuss approaches to risk management including the use of weather-index insurance options, as well as diversification of livelihoods and agricultural production, as potential responses to shocks arising from climate change. They consider adjustment of biofuel mandates and other approaches to reducing competition between food and fuel crops as a means of reducing the likelihood of shocks arising from food price volatility. In addition, they discuss the use of social safety nets and other income protection options as a response to shocks arising from natural disasters. At all times, they stress that building the resilience capacity of the food and nutrition system starts and ends with the resilience of the individuals involved. This points in particular to those groups of individuals who are discriminated against and largely excluded from participation in social, economic and political activities. For this reason, they emphasise that policies to enhance the resilience of the food and nutrition system must focus on non-discrimination in education, health and government programmes and should include policies for promoting asset ownership and human resource development and fair representation in political decision-making processes.

Another approach to these issues is to consider resilience and sustainability as a multi-dimensional phenomenon and explore the ecological and economic characteristics of a sustainable and resilient system. The aim here is to determine the limits within which the system can operate safely while ensuring that it can continue to respond to stresses and shocks; in other words, to identify the dimensions of a 'safe operating space' for the system. Building on work by Rockstrom et al. (2009), a study by Whitfield et al. (2015) discusses the role of 'sustainability spaces' in exploring the sustainability and resilience of complex agrifood systems. These studies suggest that the limited environmental and ecological capacity of systems to support economic and social activities marks the upper boundary for levels of these activities that are consistent with resilience and sustainability. A further development of these ideas considers what is required to provide satisfactory levels of social wellbeing in addition to environmental and ecological sustainability. This approach simultaneously considers a set of lower bounds on social achievement (defined by internationally agreed minimum standards for human outcomes) and upper bounds on environmental and ecological degradation defined by scientific agreement (Dearing et al., 2014; Raworth, 2012; Raworth, 2017). This indicates a need for further work, to define and characterise 'safe and just spaces' for global food production and for the global food and nutrition system and to expand notions of sustainability and resilience to encapsulate other dimensions including considerations of social justice. This could provide "a fairer, more prosperous, peaceful and sustainable world in which no one is left behind" (FAO, 2015), that promotes social cohesion in a way that supports food system sustainability and resilience.

Summary and policy implications

In this chapter, we recognise that any commitment to feed those who are hungry requires that all processes supporting food security remain stable, sustainable and resilient to shocks and stresses. This chapter, therefore, discusses the notions of stability, sustainability and resilience in relation to the three primary dimensions of food security, availability of sufficient food, individual livelihoods and food affordability, and the utilisation of food to provide adequate nutrition.

Following the increases in food prices in the latter years of the last decade, the stability of the food system and its ability to continue providing affordable food has been called into question. Yet the initial spike in food prices in 2008 subsided quickly, and subsequent sharp increases of similar magnitudes in 2011 and 2012 attracted little attention and comment. In fact, subsequent investigations of long-term changes in prices have shown that, for most food commodities, volatility of prices since 2000 has not increased above historical levels and may well have decreased. Nevertheless, a wide range of policy interventions have been investigated. These include trade and storage policies to mitigate the impact of domestic production shocks, as well as risk management policies for producers faced with anticipated volatility in market prices for inputs and well as for outputs. We also discuss policies, based on the provision of safety nets for families and households, to enable poor and vulnerable consumers to cope with the impacts of food price spikes arising from domestic or overseas markets.

Economic development activities are generally regarded as sustainable when they can provide a level of human wellbeing that does not decline over time, supported by non-declining levels of consumption, volume of production and stock of capital assets. Given that the productivity of the asset stock can increase over time as technology changes, it is possible that production (hence consumption and wellbeing) can remain constant or increase over time, even when the asset stock declines. This phenomenon has been seen as a type of 'technology tread-mill'. It is also possible that individual preferences could change over time to allow wellbeing to remain constant while levels of consumption decline, a type of 'behavioural tread-mill'.

There is general agreement that a sustainable economic system must be built on the conservation of a specific portfolio of assets rather than the stock of productive assets in aggregate. This is an explicit recognition of the fact that, for many types of important ecological assets, it is not possible to find adequate substitutes, at least in the short run, and corresponds to an ecological approach to sustainability that stresses the importance of resilience in ecological and socioeconomic systems. By focusing on the capacity of the system to deal with shocks and stresses as it continues to provide basic services, this approach provides a more general view of sustainability that can accommodate temporary setbacks.

Sustainable food security has been investigated at the global, regional and national levels and for a number of individual dimensions. For example, many studies of the sustainability of agricultural production and food availability have considered a large number of indicators of individual farming practices in assessing the sustainability and viability of agricultural production and its impacts on economic, environmental and social aspects of rural communities and society more generally. The potential viability of sustainable intensification approaches to enhancing food availability in current circumstances is also being investigated. There have also been a number of studies investigating the potential contribution of sustainable individual livelihoods to poverty reduction and the affordability of adequate food and nutrition. In addition, some studies take a broader view of the food system, accepting that individual dimensions of food and nutrition security cannot be considered in isolation when policy interventions are conceived, designed and implemented.

More recently, a number of studies have focused specifically on the resilience of the agriculture and food system, building on previous work in ecological and socioeconomic systems analysis. The aim has been to devise interventions that can be deployed to enhance coping capacity and resilience to existing and ongoing shocks and that can also reduce vulnerability to future shocks. These studies have focused on alternative approaches to measuring resilience in the provision of income and nutrition and on considering the potential impact of ecological thresholds on global food security. In addition, these studies have highlighted a need to consider how the global food system can be resilient and sustainable, while delivering outcomes that not only feed the hungry, but also promote social cohesion and meet at least the minimum requirements for social justice.

References

Abbot, P. C., Hurt, C. and Tyner, W. E. 2008. *What's Driving Food Prices?* Oak Brook, IL: Farm Foundation.

Adam, D. 2008. Food Price Rises Threaten Global Security – UN. *The Guardian.*

Arrow, K., Bolin, B., Constanza, R., Dasgupta, P., Folke, C., Holling, C. S., Jannson, B., Levin, S., Maler, K. G., Perrings, C. and Pimentel, D. 1995. Economic Growth, Carrying Capacity, and the Environment. *Science*, 268, 520–521.

Arrow, K., Dasgupta, P., Goulder, L., Daily, G., Ehrlich, P. R., Heal, G., Levin, S., Maler, K-G., Schneider, S., Starrett, D. and Walker, B. 2004. Are We Consuming Too Much? *Journal of Economic Perspectives*, 18, 147–172.

Barrett, C. B. and Constas, M. A. 2014. Toward a Theory of Resilience for International Development Applications. *Proceedings of the National Academy of Science*, 111, 14625–14630.

Barrett, C. B. and Headey, D. 2014. A Proposal for Measuring Resilience in a Risky World. *In:* Fan, S., Pandya-Lorch, R. and Yosef, S. (eds.) *Resilience for Food and Nutrition Security*. Washington, DC: International Food Policy Research Institute.

Barrientos, A. 2013. Does Vulnerability Create Poverty Traps? *In:* Shephard, A. and Brunt, J. (eds.) *Chronic Poverty: Concepts, Causes and Policy.* New York: Palgrave Macmillan.

Bellemare, M. 2014. Rising Food Prices, Food Price Volatility, and Social Unrest. *American Journal of Agricultural Economics*, 97, 1–21.

Bennett, E., Carpenter, S. R., Gordon, L. J., Ramankutty, N., Balvanera, P., Campbell, B. M., Cramer, W., Foley, J. A., Folke, C., Karlberg, L., Liu, J. G., Lotze-Campem, H., Mueller, N. D., Peterson, G. D., Polasky, S., Rockstrom, J., Scholes, R. J. and Spierenburg, M. 2014. Toward a More Resilient Agriculture. *Solutions for a Sustainable and Desirable Future*, 5, 65–75.

Benton, T. G., Fairweather, D., Graves, A., Harris, J., Jones, A., Lenton, T., Norman, R., O'riordan, T., Pope, E. and Tiffin, R. 2017. Environmental Tipping Points and Food System Dynamics: Main Report. *The Global Food Security Programme*.

Capone, R., El Bilali, H., Debs, P., Cardone, G. and Driouech, N. 2014. Food System Sustainability and Food Security: Connecting the Dots. *Journal of Food Security*, 2, 13–22.

Chambers, R. and Conway, G. R. 1992. Sustainable Rural Livelihoods: Practical Concepts for the 21st Century. *IDS Discussion Paper*. Brighton: Institute of Development Studies.

Cisse, J. D. and Barrett, C. B. 2016. *Estimating Development Resilience: A Moments-Based Approach.* Charles H. Dyson School of Applied Economics & Management. Ithaca NY: Cornell University.

Common, M. and Perrings, C. 1992. Towards an Ecological Economics of Sustainability. *Ecological Economics*, 6, 7–34.

Cooke, B. and Nobles, M. 2009. Recent Food Price Movements: A Time Series Analysis. *IFPRI Discussion Paper 00942*. Washington, DC: IFPRI.

Dasgupta, P. 2010. Nature's Role in Sustaining Economic Development. *Philosophical Transactions of the Royal Society B*, 365, 5–11.

Dearing, J. A., Wang, R., Zhang, K., Dyke, J. G., Haberl, H., Hossain, M. S., Langdon, P. G., Lenton, T. M., Raworth, K., Brown, S., Carstensen, J., Cole, M. J., Cornell, S. E., Dawson, T. P., Doncaster, C. P., Eigenbrod, F., Floerke, M., Jeffers, E., Mackay, A. W., Nykvist, B. and Poppy, G. M. 2014. Safe and Just Operating Spaces for Regional Social-Ecological Systems. *Global Environmental Change-Human and Policy Dimensions*, 28, 227–238.

Dillon, E. J., Hennessey, T., Buckley, C., Donnellan, T., Hanrahan, K., Moran, B. and Ryan, M. 2017. Measuring Progress in Agricultural Sustainability to Support Policy-Making. *International Journal of Agricultural Sustainability*, 14, 31–44.

Fan, S., Pandya-Lorch, R. and Yosef, S. (eds.) 2014. *Resilience for Food and Nutrition Security.* Washington, DC: International Food Policy Research Institute.

FAO. 2013. *Resilient Livelihoods: Disaster Risk Reduction for Food and Nutrition Security.* Rome: FAO.

FAO. 2015. FAO and the 17 Sustainable Development Goals. Rome: FAO

FAO, IFAD and WFP. 2011. *The State of Food Insecurity in the World 2011: How Does International Price Volatility Affect Domestic Economics and Food Security?* Rome: FAO.

Folke, C. 2006. Resilience: The Emergence of a Perspective for Social-Ecological Systems Analyses. *Global Environmental Change*, 16, 253–267.

Folke, C., Carpenter, C., Elmqvist, T., Gunderson, L., Holling, C. S. and Walker, B. 2002. Resilience and Sustainable Development: Building Adaptive Capacity in a World of Transformations. *AMBIO*, 31, 437–440.

Garnett, T. 2014. Three Perspectives on Sustainable Food Security: Efficiency, Demand Restraint, Food System Transformation. What Role for Life Cycle Assessment? *Journal of Cleaner Production*, 73, 10–18.

Garnett, T., Appleby, M. C., Balmford, A., Batemen, I. J., Benton, T. G., Bloomer, P., Burlingame, B., Dawkins, M., Dolan, L., Fraser, D., Herrero, M., Hoffman, I., Smith, P.,

Thornton, P. K., Toulmin, C., Vermeulen, S. J. and Godfray, H. C. J. 2013. Sustainable Intensification in Agriculture: Premises and Policies. *Sciences*, 341, 33–34.

Gilbert, C. L. 2010. How to Understand High Food Process. *Journal of Agricultural Economics*, 61, 398–425.

Gilbert, C. L. and Morgan, C. W. 2010. Food Price Volatility. *Philosophical Transaction of the Royal Society B*, 365, 3023–3034.

Godfray, H. C. J. 2015. The Debate Over Sustainable Intensification. *Food Security*, 7, 199–208.

Godfray, H. C. J. and Garnett, T. 2014. Food Security and Sustainable Intensification. *Philosophical Transactions of the Royal Society B-Biological Sciences*, 369., 1–10.

Krantz, L. 2001. *The Sustainable Livelihood Approach to Poverty Reduction.* Stockholm: Swedish International Development Cooperation Agency.

Latruffe, L., Diazabakana, A., Bockstaller, C., Desjeux, Y., Finn, J., Kelly, E., Ryan, M. and Uthes, S. 2016. Measurement of Sustainability in Agriculture: A Review of Indicators. *Studies in Agricultural Economics*, 118, 123–130.

Levin, S. A., Barrett, S., Aniyar, S., Baumol, W. J., Bliss, C., Bolin, B., Dasgupta, P., Ehrlich, P., Folke, C., Gren, I-M., Holling, C. S., Jansson, A-M., Jansson, B-O., Martin, D., Maler, K-G., Perrings, C. and Sheshinsky, E. 1998. Resilience in Natural and Socioeconomic Systems. *Environment and Development Economics*, 3, 222–234.

Morduch, J. 1994. Poverty and Vulnerability. *The American Economic Review*, 84, 221–225.

Norton, B. G. and Toman, M. A. 1997. Sustainability: Ecological and Economic Perspectives. *Land Economics*, 73, 553–568.

Office of Food for Peace. 2015. *2016–2025 Food Assistance and Food Security Strategy.* Washington, DC: USAID.

Pearce, D. W. and Atkinson, G. D. 1993. Capital Theory and the Measurement of Sustainable Development: Some Empirical Evidence. *Ecological Economics*, 8, 103–108.

Perrings, C. 2006. Resilience and Sustainable Development. *Environment and Development Economics*, 11, 417–427.

Pezzey, J. 1992. Sustainability: An Interdisciplinary Guide. *Environmental Values*, 1, 321–362.

Piesse, J. and Thirtle, C. 2009. Three Bubbles and a Panic: An Explanatory Review of Recent Food Commodity Price Events. *Food Policy*, 34, 119–129.

Ravallion, M. 1988. Expected Poverty Under Risk-Induced Welfare Variability. *The Economic Journal*, 98, 1171–1182.

Raworth, K. 2012. A Safe and Just Space for Humanity: Can We Live Within the Doughnut? *Oxfam Discussion Paper*.

Raworth, K. 2017. *Doughnut Economics: Seven Ways to Think Like a 21st-Century Economist.* London: Random House Business.

Reisch, L., Eberle, U. and Lorek, S. 2013. Sustainable Food Consumption: An Overview of Contemporary Issues and Policies. *Sustainability: Science, Practice, and Policy*, 9, 7–25.

Rigby, D., Woodhouse, P., Young, T. and Burton, M. 2001. Constructing a Farm Level Indicator of Sustainable Agricultural Practice. *Ecological Economics*, 39, 463–478.

Rockstrom, J., Steffen, W., Noone, K., Persson, A., Chapin, III, F. S., Lambin, E. F., Lenton, T. M., Scheffer, M., Folke, C., Schellnhuber, H. J., Nykvist, B., De Wit, C. A., Hughes, T., Van Der Leeuw, S., Rodhe, H., Sverker, S., Snyder, P. K., Constanza, R., Svedin, U., Falkenmark, M., Karlberg, L., Corell, R. W., Fabry, V. J., Hansen, J., Walker,

B., Liverman, D., Richardson, K., Crutzen, P. J. and Foley, J. A. 2009. A Safe Operating Space for Humanity. *Nature*, 461, 472–475.

Sharma, D. and Sharendu, S. 2011. Assessing Farm-Level Agricultural Sustainability Over a 60-Year Period in Rural Eastern India. *Environmentalist*, 31, 325–337.

Smerlak, M. and Vaitla, B. 2017. A Non-Equilibrium Formulation of Food Security Resilience. *Royal Society Open Science*, 4., 1–10.

Tadasse, G., Algieri, B., Kalkuhl, M. and Von Braun, J. 2016. Drivers and Triggers of International Food Price Spikes and Volatility. *In:* Kalkuhl, M., Von Braun, J. and Torero, M. (eds.) *Food Price Volatility and Its Implications for Food Security and Policy.* Basel, Switzerland: Springer International.

Tendall, D. M., Joerin, J., Kopainsky, B., Edwards, P., Shreck, A., Le, Q. B., Kruetli, P., Grant, M. and Six, J. 2015. Food System Resilience: Defining the Concept. *Global Food Security*, 6, 17–23.

Vermeir, I. and Verbeke, W. 2006. Sustainable Food Consumption: Exploring the Consumer "Attitude – Behavioural Intention" Gap. *Journal of Agricultural and Environmental Ethics*, 19, 169–194.

Victor, P. A. 1991. Indicators of Sustainable Development: Some Lessons From Capital Theory. *Ecological Economics*, 4, 191–214.

WCED. 1987. *Our Common Future.* New York: World Commission on Environment and Development.

Whitfield, S., Benton, T. G., Dallimer, M., Firbank, L. G., Poppy, G. M., Sallu, S. M. and Stringer, L. C. 2015. Sustainability Spaces for Complex Agri-Food Systems. *Food Security*, 7, 1291–1297.

Woller, G., Wolfe, J. M., Brand, M., Fowler, B., Parrot, L., Thompson, J., Dempsey, J., Berkowitz, L. and Van Haeften, B. 2011. *Livelihood and Food Security Conceptual Framework.* Washington, DC: USAID Livelihood and Food Security Technical Assistance Project.

Wright, B. 2014a. Data at Our Fingertips, Myths in Our Minds: Recent Grain Price Jumps as the 'Perfect Storm'. *Australian Journal of Agricultural and Resource Economics*, 58, 538–553.

Wright, B. 2014b. Global Biofuels: Key to the Puzzle of Grain Market Behaviour. *Journal of Economic Perspectives*, 28, 73–98.

Zseleczky, L. and Yosef, S. 2014. Are Shocks Becoming More Frequent or Intense? *In:* Fan, S., Pandya-Lorch, R. and Yosef, S. (eds.) *Resilience for Food and Nutrition Security.* Washington, DC: International Food Policy Research Institute.

7   Summary and conclusions

Feeding the hungry: a summary of problems and prospects

The problems of hunger and malnutrition remain a major concern for many millions of people worldwide, despite the evident success of our attempts to expand the productivity of the global food production system and enhance its ability to provide sufficient food as the global population expands and diets change in response to increased prosperity. Another puzzling aspect of the current global food and nutrition problem is simultaneous undernutrition and overconsumption, starvation and obesity, often in the same country and even in the same city. In addition, there is increasing evidence that significant amounts of edible food are being wasted by wholesalers, retailers and especially by households. Yet this triple dilemma of hunger in the face of adequate production, coincident starvation and obesity and ever-increasing food waste is an oversimplification of the complex interactions that underpin our food production and consumption activities. As we suggested in the introductory chapter, this book is an attempt to explore these complex relationships from an economics perspective.

The number of hungry people in the world has declined steadily over recent decades, providing a measure of progress in achieving two internationally agreed targets for hunger reduction. The World Food Summit in 1996 agreed ". . . to eradicate hunger in all countries, with an immediate view of reducing the number of undernourished people to half their present level no later than 2015". The second target derives from the Millennium Development Goals; MDG Goal 1 had a target of cutting by half the proportion of people suffering from hunger by 2015. The fact that both these targets have been missed makes it essential that we consider how we might make more substantive progress in the context of the next set of international goals, the Sustainable Development Goals, launched in January 2016. Goal 1 (ending poverty) and Goal 2 (achieving zero hunger) are of particular interest here.

We explore the current state of food security across the world (Chapter 2) and the alternative metrics used to establish the scale of the hunger problem and identify the characteristics of those who are hungry. As well as highlighting potential difficulties with currently popular measures of hunger and food insecurity, this chapter emphasises that these problems are characterised by a number of overlapping dimensions. Following common practice in contemporary studies of these issues, four dimensions are examined here, food availability, food affordability, food utilisation and nutrition, and stability/sustainability/resilience in each of these dimensions.

The first dimension addresses issues related to the availability of sufficient food and the capacity of the global food production system to deliver increases in production. These increases are needed to keep pace with increasing food demand arising from global population growth, from changing diets arising through increased prosperity and other factors (the nutrition transition), and from expanding non-food demands for food crops arising from biofuel mandates and other changes. In Chapter 3, we assess our ability to expand food production to meet these demands in the face of limited land and water, changes in climate and potential constraints on the availability of other inputs, such as fertilisers and chemicals.

The food affordability dimension addresses issues that arise when individuals are not able to obtain food, in the market or by other legal means, even when there are adequate amounts of food available. This emphasises that food security is about being able to afford adequate amounts of food, rather than that food is adequately available for consumption. This shifts the focus from the food production system and resource productivity to issues related to the livelihoods of consumers, and to factors that influence livelihoods. After critically reviewing the entitlements approach and evidence for the existence of poverty traps, Chapter 4 considers a range of policy options that focus on the needs of individuals, and provide short-term hunger relief as well as medium-term and longer-term support for livelihoods.

The food utilisation and nutrition dimension highlights the importance of using food available in the household to best advantage for adequate and appropriate nutrition. A variety of issues is subsumed under this topic, including those related to micronutrient deficiency and so-called hidden hunger as well as issues of nutrition and individual productivity. This chapter also considers issues related to the nutrition transition discussed earlier, focusing on the spread of obesity and the related epidemic of non-communicable lifestyle diseases. The case for government intervention to reduce the harmful effects of these changes is also considered. In addition, Chapter 5 investigates food loss and waste, discusses its distribution across the globe and possible causes, and suggests potential approaches for learning more about this problem and designing interventions to reduce its impacts on food and nutrition security.

The final dimension introduces issues that relate to the stability, sustainability and resilience of factors underpinning the other three dimensions. The volatility of food prices, highlighted by the price spikes in 2008, 2011 and 2012, is considered in some detail, including the disruption to food markets that generated social disturbance in a significant number of cities across the world. Yet some studies suggest that these price movements were not out of line with historic price variability. However, since the factors that may have generated these price movements are still potentially active, the availability of policy measures to stabilise prices, including those related to market information and trade regulation, must be an essential part of any strategy to support food and nutrition security into the future. The sustainability of economic activities is discussed at some length, including recent studies of sustainable food security and the need to enhance both the sustainability and the resilience of the food system to promote food and nutrition security for all individuals. The chapter finishes with a brief discussion of studies that include impacts on social cohesion alongside impacts on sustainability and resilience by considering the characteristics of "safe and just operating spaces" for global and regional food systems.

Potential policy interventions

Secure food availability requires a balance between the amounts of food produced and food required. This suggests a two-pronged approach to designing policy interventions that are targeted at improving this dimension of food security: interventions that promote increases in food production on the one hand, and those that focus on managing changes in food demand on the other.

While we recognise that population growth is a key driver of food demand, we must also recognise that at current levels of global economic development and with the continuing upward trajectory of per capita incomes across all countries and regions, population growth is only one of a number of factors that is leading to ever-increasing demands for food. We must also consider the way in which preferred diets are evolving towards increasing reliance on fats and sugars, livestock and dairy products, fresh vegetables and vegetable oils, while evolving away from the traditional reliance on cereals, roots and tubers. This very significant transition is currently being observed in food consumption in many countries, especially those where the majority of the population have up to now relied on the more traditional diets. It has important implications for overall levels of food production, especially the production of grains as these now have the dual task of feeding humans directly and also providing feed for animals to meet the increasing demand for dairy and livestock products. Significantly, the principal driver of this transition is not population growth, but the increasing incomes and affluence of individuals being generated by global economic growth and the increasing urbanisation of the global population. While demand management policies have traditionally focused on population control measures, emphasis has been shifting to measures that seek to modify the impact of the nutrition transition, for example, by emphasising the importance of healthy diets, by imposing taxes on unhealthy food products and by providing subsidies for products deemed part of a healthy diet.

Over the past five decades, agricultural production has proven more than adequate in meeting this increase in food demand, even in the face of increases generated by population growth, increasing affluence, and bioenergy policies and mandates. In fact, food production in terms of kilocalories energy per capita has increased by around 40 per cent since the 1960s. Nevertheless, most academics and policy makers would suggest that food availability must continue as a priority when it comes to policy design and policy decisions, since it supports all other dimensions of food security, and there is broad support and experience for policy design and implementation in this area. There is a very wide range of policies that promote the increasing availability of food, through enhancing production capacity by improving the availability and productivity of resources, through improving the management and efficiency of food production and through facilitating the operation and stability of trade and market systems.

The persistence of hunger in the face of increasing food availability may point to a serious problem in how our economic systems are operating, but it also points to the inadequacy of considering and analysing food security problems purely in terms of food supply and availability. The missing element is recognising that lack of food affordability and effective demand for food is another key determinant of hunger. This focuses attention on the incomes of individuals and the livelihoods that support these incomes as well as the stability of food markets and the prices in these markets. Given the continuing increase in incomes and affluence arising from global economic expansion and growth, the persistence of issues related to food affordability calls into question the processes of income distribution and the extent to which the proceeds of economic growth are being shared equitably between all groups of people within individual economies. From our discussion of the entitlements approach in Chapter 4, there are two principal implications for policy interventions.

Firstly, this approach highlights the need to explore alternative means of directly supporting the livelihoods of individuals when they cannot afford to consume sufficient food to avoid undernutrition and hunger. A wide range of interventions has been implemented here. These include the introduction of social security safety nets for individuals who cannot earn sufficient income, the use of food subsidies targeted to those on low incomes, and work-for-food programmes.

Secondly, this analysis draws attention to the reasons why livelihood failure occurs in the first place and so to the underlying forces that lead to individuals not being able to afford sufficient food. This shifts the target for intervention to the factors that influence livelihoods of affected individuals, suggesting that policies should be aimed at enhancing the resource endowment of these individuals so that they are in a position to earn sufficient income (or command sufficient food entitlements) to avoid undernutrition and hunger. These policies will include those focused on education and skills (enhancing human capital), as well as those that focus more directly on business enterprise development (such as programmes to encourage investment in agriculture and rural business). They also include policies seeking broader institutional reform that encourages individuals to become more economically active (making property rights more secure, reducing corruption) and reduce political and social exclusion. The use of targeted conditional or unconditional cash transfers, with longer durations than typical safety net payments, is now becoming an increasingly popular means of facilitating effective food demand and encouraging broader economic participation.

The efficient utilisation of available affordable food to deliver satisfactory nutrition to people is also considered. Policies to encourage provision of water and sanitation infrastructure as well as basic health care are the starting point for interventions here. Other interventions might include education in nutrition management, the use of micronutrient fortification and supplementation schemes to deal with hidden hunger, the use of nutrition information, as well as taxes and subsidies to combat obesity, and policies to reduce food waste.

A different set of policies is indicated when considering stability, sustainability and resilience. Market stabilisation policies are a part of this suite of policies. While direct intervention in markets via buffer stock policies is not currently favoured, a wider range of regulatory and institutional policies that address some of the causes of market instability are still warranted. Policies are also needed that address sustainability in food production and the livelihoods of food producers and policies for enhancing the resilience to shocks and stresses in the productivity, affordability and utilisation of food.

Finding a way forward

In this final section we offer some general guidance about how policies for food and nutrition security might evolve over the near future.

Firstly, we suggest that policies for food and nutrition should reflect measures of food insecurity that are based on nutritional outcomes for individuals, families and households, rather than measures of aggregate food availability or calorie consumption. Secondly, policies for food and nutrition security should support a shift in emphasis from the availability and affordability of food, to the security, sustainability and resilience of the whole system for food and nutrition.

Out of these considerations emerge suggestions for a targeted multi-phase approach that, where and when appropriate, seeks to ensure not only relief from current hunger but also provides resources to support continuing food availability, livelihoods that enable sufficient exchange entitlements to purchase food, and appropriate facilities and incentives to ensure efficient food utilisation.

These suggestions point to interventions that consider the problems and needs of individuals, families and households, rather than political or social concerns that are observed and managed at an aggregate level. This encourages a focus on hunger and undernutrition as it affects individuals, especially the young and the vulnerable. It also focuses attention on the assets and incomes of individuals and households, as well as on the empowerment and inclusion of individuals and groups who may be disadvantaged by, and excluded from, political decisions that address allocation of public funding and resources for the provision of education, health care and basic social insurance.

A key point emerging from the analysis is the possibility and desirability of pursuing policies and designing interventions that can simultaneously contribute to the problems currently facing the food and nutrition system over more than one dimension of food and nutrition security.

For example, with the majority of hungry people residing in rural areas, interventions that target smallholder agricultural productivity can serve a double purpose in this regard. On the one hand, they lead to increases in the supply of food available on the market thereby damping any tendency for prices to rise, while on the other hand, they have the potential for increasing incomes and employment (and food entitlements) for the smallholders themselves and any additional workers they may wish to employ. This type of policy could also include incentives to increase purchased inputs as well as the provision of improved systems for marketing agricultural products and for the provision of credit to farmers. The provision of rural infrastructure is also crucial, including roads, storage depots and irrigation networks. In addition, these policies can include supporting additional research for the development of improved agricultural techniques, crop varieties and breeds of animals specifically suited for smallholder agriculture, as well as the education and extension systems that make these improvements available at farm level. They can also include measures that encourage the production of high-quality output and the efficient use of inputs. On a broader basis, policies to facilitate secure tenure and access to land are also important.

Where these policies cannot effectively provide employment for all who need a sustainable livelihood, more broadly targeted policies for poverty alleviation may be called for, particularly policies focused on increasing the number of jobs available to poor people and increasing their productivity in undertaking these jobs. This latter implies increasing the amount of 'capital' that these people can bring to these jobs, for example, through enhanced skills and expertise (investment in 'human capital') or through access to credit facilities. Enhancing human capital requires significant investment in education and training that is carefully targeted to be accessible to the potentially hungry population (and can be taken up without compromising already precarious livelihoods) and delivers skills that are readily marketable in the locality.

Policy interventions to enhance food utilisation, or to improve the stability, sustainability or resilience of the food and nutrition system, can also serve a double purpose. For example, policies that set out to encourage healthy eating can help reduce the consumption of livestock products in a way that reduces the demand for cereals and increases food availability; policies that reduce food loss and waste also contribute directly to food availability. The double impact of policies for stability, sustainability and resilience arises principally from policies that seek to reduce the risk faced by producers and consumers, such as cash transfers, insurance schemes and other policies for risk reduction. Firstly, by reducing risk for producers, these interventions encourage increased use of inputs and increased investment, leading directly to increased production and food availability. Secondly, cash transfers to consumers will also increase market entitlements and food affordability.

What this means is that policy intervention strategies for feeding the hungry should provide broad based support for all four dimensions of food and nutrition security, seeking to enhance the sustainability and resilience of the food and nutrition system while promoting social cohesion by protecting justice and dignity for all hungry people.

Index

For Product Safety Concerns and Information please contact our EU
representative GPSR@taylorandfrancis.com
Taylor & Francis Verlag GmbH, Kaufingerstraße 24, 80331 München, Germany

www.ingramcontent.com/pod-product-compliance
Ingram Content Group UK Ltd.
Pitfield, Milton Keynes, MK11 3LW, UK
UKHW020946180425
457613UK00019B/542